ASK STEVE

"The growth in popularity of bed-and breakfasts as an alternative to expensive hotels has caused many a home or apartment owner to cast a speculative eye around unused bedrooms to see if they can be put to profitable use. There are many aspects to consider— everything from putting a little extra starch in the curtains to zoning and licensing regulations. It might be very helpful to read a book or two on the subject. One good one is 'How to Start Your Own Bed & Breakfast' by Mary Zander. This book guides readers through an explanation of B&B establishment, zoning regula- tions, health and sanitary considerations, publicizing, market- ing, etc. The book also describes the function of reservation ser- vice organizations (RSOs) and explains how they can be of service in matching guests up with B&B hosts. The back of the book provides a listing of many of these organizations. . . ."

> Steve Birnbaum, Good Housekeeping Travel
> Editor, in his syndicated column as it
> appeared in the *Houston Post, New York
> Daily News,* and other papers.

How to Start Your Own
BED
&
BREAKFAST

How to Start Your Own
BED
&
BREAKFAST

A Guide to Hosting Paying Guests
in Your House or Apartment

by Mary Zander

GOLDEN HILL PRESS · SPENCERTOWN, NEW YORK

Library of Congress Catalogue Card Number: 85-80565
    ISBN: 0-9614876-0-7

Published in the United States by Golden Hill Press,
    Box 122, Spencertown, New York 12165
Printed in the United States by Studley Press, Dalton, Massachusetts
Text Illustrations by Margaret Eberle. Cover by Emily McCully.
Brochure Illustration by Leslie Cooley.

TO ISABEL,
An octagenarian host whose gentle and
benevolent hospitality has touched many guests,

and

TO HELEN,
With whom we have shared so much, and
who would have enjoyed this book.

. . . *"I spoke of a wider hospitality than that of your house," said
Phoebus. "I spoke of the hospitality of the heart."*
Elizabeth Goudge

Contents

Preface

This book guides you step-by-step through the process of starting and operating your own Bed and Breakfast. It is designed to save you time and money, while helping you make the basic decisions.

Everything we present here need not be applied to every B&B. The widest range of information is intended for the host who has several rooms to rent and wants to undertake her or his own publicity and marketing in a high-volume business. The more casual or intermittant host, or the apartment dweller, will not need to do so many things. The potential innkeeper or reservation service operator (RSO), on the other hand, may wish to utilize most of the material. As you read along, you can choose, adapt and apply what is most relevant to your particular needs.

You should also, as you go through the book, begin to see the fun and enjoyment that is a part of B&B. It is an agreeable, sometimes delightful way to make extra income. Yet, it is not difficult to begin, there is no large capital outlay, it can be done from your home and, to a large extent, you control the amount of time you spend on it.

You should, however, approach it as seriously as you would any other business venture. Make no hasty decisions. Plan carefully. Talk to others in your household who would directly or indirectly be involved. When you have decided, begin slowly. A solid base makes for a successful B&B.

Finally, as you get underway, we wish you the good times with your B&B that we have had with ours.

Acknowledgements

Experience and material for a book of this kind come from so many different sources that it is difficult to note everyone who directly or indirectly helps with such an undertaking. I am grateful to all those persons who have, even unknowingly, shared ideas and experiences with me.

I thank the many B&B guests and the hosts from whom I have learned; and my neighbors who shared hosting experiences with me. Thanks to all the good people who gave their recipes and are noted in Chapter 7. Thanks also to Helen Sacco of the Columbia County Chamber of Commerce and to Sheryl Woods of the New York State Department of Tourism for their helpful interviews about various aspects of B&B in our area.

Lorna Moore, Ellen Berry, Marilyn Mesick, Ralph and Ruth Sleight and Lorraine Zagarola have read and critiqued the manuscript, and Lorna Moore gave further editorial assistance. Margaret Eberle created the illustrations, and Emily McCully the cover. Charles Kleinbaum and Lawrence Zagarola gave technical assistance with the manuscript. A particular thank you to Thelma Hall for manuscript typing and production assistance, as well as for good advice. Thanks to Sara Freed for jacket copy and editorial advice; to Stuart Murray for editorial and production assistance; and to Thomas Reardon for knowledgeable help with book production.

A special thanks to Paula Treder for her support and encouragement, to Glen and Ralphina Kistler, to Isabel Zander and, most gratefully, to Lorraine Zagarola, who has assisted in so many phases of this undertaking.

Thank you all.

Introduction

Bed and Breakfast has at last come of age in the United States. More and more people are hosting B&Bs, and the number of guidebooks, reservation service organizations (RSOs) and listings for B&B lodgings has snowballed. It is now relatively easy for guests to find the B&B they want and for hosts to find the guests they want.

Not only have B&Bs caught on as a cheaper alternative to hotels and motels, but many provide an elegant and different traveling experience. And, whether posh or modest, all are special, because no two are alike. The location, the kind of house or apartment, the personality of the hosts—each imparts its own unique ambience. So, to growing numbers of travelers, B&B is now the "in" way to go.

This trend has not been unnoticed by the media. News sources as varied as the *Wall Street Journal* and the *AARP News Bulletin* discuss B&B as a new money-making phenomenon. *Good Housekeeping*, *Women's Day* and *Ladies Home Journal* tout B&B as a way to make money while staying home. Travel columns in the

New York Times, Chicago Tribune and the *Los Angeles Times* catalog the growing number of B&B guidebooks and reservation service agencies. *Yankee, Sunset, Americana* and *New York* magazines, the *Better Homes and Gardens* magazine, *Country Home* and the American Express magazine, *Travel and Leisure,* run articles—often enticingly illustrated with photographs of gorgeous rooms or houses—featuring B&B as a travel alternative.

State departments of tourism and local chambers of commerce are promoting B&B because it brings new money into their areas. Travel agents nationwide now supply guests for B&B booking agencies. Real estate sections of local newspapers market homes as being "ideal for Bed and Breakfast."

While the trend still is for B&B lodgings of the one or two room variety, there are—probably due to the increasing popularity of restoring older houses and buildings—more large B&Bs which call themselves B&B inns. Indeed, some hosts have used the small B&B as a trial run to learn some of the elements of country innkeeping without having to invest the time, money and physical energy required to run a profitable inn that also serves meals.

Whatever your personal goal—B&B host, innkeeper or reservation service operator—there is a place for you within this rapidly expanding little industry. You will, however, need guidance in selecting the operational alternatives appropriate to your particular needs. You can be big or small, independent, or intertwined with others, but should define clearly where you want to go with your B&B before you commit yourself.

The chapters of this book follow the order in which you will need to make decisions as you shape your B&B. We begin with the elementary whats, whos, wheres and whys.

PART I
Making the Decision to Become a B&B Host

1
What is
Bed and Breakfast?

In its simplest form, Bed and Breakfast means providing for a fee a bedroom, a bathroom—usually shared—and a continental breakfast.

There are many variations to these basics. If the house is a big one with several spare bedrooms, guests will share breakfast and bathroom with other travelers. If the hosts are particularly interested in meeting people, they may invite guests for drinks or dinners. Most do not restrict guests to bedroom areas, and will offer the use of the living room, family room, backyard or balcony.

Homes vary too. Some are quite modest; some positively palatial. Some are old-fashioned; some ultra modern. Many offer only one room; some are large enough to be called inns. A surprising number are in apartments in the midst of major cities; others are on farms or in small hamlets from New England to the West Coast. Some are on boats; some in bungalows. At least one is in a lighthouse.

Most hosts offer the traditional continental breakfast of roll, juice and coffee, but some have house specialties which they serve as part of a full breakfast. Activities also vary. Antique shopping, swimming, concert-going, hunting, tennis, whalewatching, museum hopping, applepicking, bird-watching and golf are a sampling of those available to the B&B guest. The range of places to stay and things to do has as many faces and flavors as the country itself.

Who are the Hosts?

All kinds of people. As with homes, variety is the thing. Some hosts are retirees or middle-aged people whose children have grown and gone. They may have large houses which are costly to heat and maintain, and renting some of those empty rooms is an enjoyable way to help pay such expenses. Many are young people who have bought and remodeled older, perhaps historic houses, and who rent some of the rooms to offset the costs.

City hosts offer B&B guests a safe haven in the anonymous urban environment, with accommodations in spare rooms of large apartments, or even in their own bedrooms, if they are away. Other hosts own working farms with lots of space for people to ride, hike or ski across. Some are people who have bought a city or country house with extra rooms and plan an early retirement cushioned by B&B income.

Some hosts are home all day and can spend time on their guests. Others—especially city people—have regular, full-time jobs, and B&B hosting is their evening or weekend occupation. Some even let their unhosted apartments through B&B booking agencies and may never meet their guests. More women than men are presently hosting, but many more couples and single men are doing so now than before. The one characteristic most hosts do have in common is a genuine enjoyment of people.

Who are the Guests?

Typical B&B guests also are likely to be people who enjoy meeting others. And, although some of them may be attracted by the lower cost of B&B accommodations, others are looking for a really elegant travel experience and will pay a premium price for it. Some are business travelers wanting a change from expensive or routine accommodations. Some are single women who feel more secure in a private home than in an anonymous hotel room. Many are foreign visitors, who, accustomed to B&Bs in Europe, use them in the United States in order to meet Americans and learn more about them. Lots more are couples or families on vacation who like and seek out B&B lodgings.

Guests from out-of-town usually turn up through guidebook listings or reservation service organizations (RSOs). From local sources, typical guests include the overflow from weddings, funerals, family reunions, and holiday gatherings, when local families do not have enough room. Conferences or conventions may provide guests. A family, or group, such as hunters, may seek reasonable accommodations through B&B. If you are listed in the Yellow Pages you will get last-minute calls from people who have not the foggiest notion what B&B is, but are desperate for a place to stay because all the local motels are filled.

Whatever the kinds of guests who come your way, the likelihood is that you will enjoy them. While every guest certainly does not become an instant friend, our own experiences—as well as those of other hosts we know—include pleasant visits where strangers started on the road to friendship, good conversation was shared, and everyone felt richer for it.

This is the real bonus of Bed and Breakfast, beyond that of the host making money and the guest getting an accommodation for a reasonable amount. Visitors are made to feel comfortable in new places, nice houses are saved from deterioration and hosts and guest share glimpses of other people's lives and dreams. Not a bad way to spend a weekend!

2
Evaluating
Your Own Situation

The suitability of your home for B&B use is determined not just by the home itself, but by its location, and by the personality of you, its host.

Your Location

Any location is workable as a B&B accommodation, but a good location is an important element of a very successful B&B. If you are aiming for a steady income from a high volume of guests, then either you must have a location with good pulling power or you must understand and do what needs to be done to give it better pulling power. If your goal is having only occasional guests, location is not as important.

Is your area one which usually appeals to vacationers because of swimming and watersports, skiing, scenery, concerts, or seasonal attractions like autumn foliage? Or, are you in or fairly near the center of a major city? Then you are very well-situated. If not, are there one or more things about your location that you can use in attracting guests? For instance, are you near a superhighway exit where people might want to stay when they stop driving for the night? Would the real estate brokers near you be glad to have overnight lodgings for weekend homeseekers?

Is yours an area with homes, sites or museums of architectural or historic interest? A hunting or fishing area? Are there schools, or colleges, or hospitals nearby that attract visitors? Or, could your B&B be one of the few places to stay in an area that has almost no overnight accommodations? Are you in a comparatively safe neighborhood in the suburbs or in a "bedroom borough" of a major city?

Most houses or apartments have one or more such selling points to their location. There may even be attractions in your area that you are not aware of; do your homework. For some of you, making the most of your location means doing very little; for others it will mean enhancing your location by playing up its most appealing aspects in your preparation and publicity.

Your Home

Your house or apartment does not have to be big or impressive. It truly can be modest, but it does have to function well as a guest accommodation. Is there at least one room sufficiently private for guests to feel comfortable? Can it be easily set up to function as a guest room?

Take a long, hard look at the room or rooms you are proposing to use. Judge them on their own merits. Do not make irrelevant comparisons with someone else's home or one of those fabulous B&B pictures in the magazines. That will mislead you. We are not talking here about how *fancy* your home is. We mean you should examine everyday things like mattresses, rugs, and closet space—

the things you take for granted because you are used to them.

Is the room clean, functional and somewhat attractive? Or can you with relatively little expense or none at all make it so? With how much effort? Apply the same gimlet eye to the bathroom guests will use. Try to assess how it looks to a stranger. Does it need new paint, new wallpaper, a new toilet seat? Or are the old ones okay? Is the bathroom easily accessible to guests? Will the hot water system accommodate several people taking showers or baths in quick succession? Finally, is your home usually free of clutter or can it be shaped up to be so?

Beyond these basics, are there things that make the house or apartment a little more distinctive? A patio; a balcony; a fireplace; a cozy family room; a sunporch; a yard or garden; a nice place to walk or hike? Is it furnished in some special way, perhaps with antiques or period furniture? Does it have pleasant views of hills, or parks, or city streets? Did you design or build it yourself? Is it old, or does it have a history? Are there features of your home that, if played up, might be of interest to strangers?

Although any place can function as a B&B, common sense tells you that if yours has one or more such features plus a good location, it will have greater appeal. A very attractive location can help a modest home, and an impressive or distinctive home can help a less interesting location.

You as Host

Only you can honestly evaluate yourself. Do you truly feel you will enjoy meeting people and sharing your home with them? Or do you feel at ease only with people very much like yourself? Are you worried about your possessions? Are you nervous and suspicious about having strangers in your home? Then you should not be a host. Your unease and lack of enjoyment will be apparent to your guests; you will be doing something you do not enjoy, and the venture will not be successful or pleasant. You must have an easy and open attitude about people if you are to play the host to the mutual satisfaction of yourself, your guests and your family.

Whether your goal is to have B&B guests occasionally or on a regular basis, you need to commit yourself to an organized plan, however minimal. Such commitment does not mean that you are on hand at all times—many hosts work full or part time and are only evening or weekend or occasional hosts. It does mean that you will run a shipshape place; keep it clean and attractive; make your guests feel welcome in a home that is efficiently run; be there when you say you will; and respond promptly to guest phone calls and letters.

Do you, or others who will be involved, have the energy and motivation to deal with these things? Who is going to promptly respond to inquiries, check the mail, do the laundry, prepare breakfast and answer the phone? Now is the time to weigh all these factors and how they apply to you, and arrive at an estimate of the effort needed to make your place the kind of B&B you want.

Think it over. Does it sound good to you? Do you still want to be a B&B host? If so, the next step is to lay the groundwork needed for your own B&B.

PART II
Groundwork

3

Readying Your Home

The major factors to be considered in getting your home ready are: cleanliness and attractiveness; function and comfort; safety, and, if applicable, special features.

You should assign priorities. First goals are to be clean and functional. Extra degrees of attractiveness can come later, and must be weighed against the time, effort and money it takes to achieve them.

Those of you having homes that are distinctive and elegant will be on surer ground, but most of us will not know quite how we stack up, and against what standards, when we come to assess how our own homes appear to others. It is hard to achieve perspective.

Be Yourself

As you look over your home, you will recognize an ambience that is specifically related to you, your life-style, your personal tastes. It is, for example, utilitarian, charming, rustic, warm, coolly modern, cozy, homey or elegant. Whatever your B&B goal and whatever preparation you do, always value and emphasize your own tone and lifestyle. Don't work against it. It is a part of your strength. "Doing what comes naturally" is easy. Don't try to affect some tone alien to yourself but one which you hope is appealing to others. You may lose your way and weaken the product: your B&B. Remember that it is supposed to be fun, not worrisome, to show off your home.

Beginning hosts sometimes tend to be self-conscious and want to do too much in preparation. Try to develop some objectivity. Have friends help you look things over when deciding what has to be done to get ready. Or, if you are considering being listed with an RSO, ask them to send a representative to help you evaluate your home.

Generally speaking, expend no more time and money than is necessary until you see what kind of volume you do. If you have a great location, you can be clean and functional without emphasizing attractiveness or special features and still be in demand as a B&B. If you're aiming for a high-volume business, or your location is not prime, you may want to do a bit more.

Cleanliness

Rooms get tired. Take a look around and see what you can do with simple maintenance and cleaning before you start massive redecorating. Are there places in the house—especially in the guest room or bath—that are really dingy and need washing or a touch-up coat of paint? Do you need to paste up a peeling bit of paper? Are the lamp shades grey-looking? Are there cobwebs under the bed?

Washing and drycleaning slipcovers and bedspreads, washing

windows and curtains, polishing floors, very thorough vacuuming and dusting, all add to the clean look that must underlie whatever else you are trying to achieve. We spruced up all our wooden furniture by washing it with Murphy's Soap, which comes in paste or liquid form. Then we polished everything with Formby's furniture polish. Repeating such a procedure as needed keeps old furniture looking good, minimizes scratches and makes the finish glow. The overall effect is to brighten the room.

The bathroom must have a good going over. Touch-up painting should be done if needed. Toilet, tub, shower, shower curtains, mirrors, rugs, pipes, and all the tiny corners should be spotlessly clean. This room really should shine. If it is shared with the hosts, their personal items should be removed or put away in the medicine cabinet. Go over this room with an eagle eye. A clean bathroom is an absolute necessity.

Remember that clean means no clutter—that the guest room be free of extraneous materials such as family belongings. If they must be there, they should be stored in the backs of closets or in the bottom drawer of the dresser. Don't leave them highly visible under the beds. It really is preferable that they be removed from the room.

While special attention is given to the guest room and bath, the other parts of the house open to guests need similar treatment. And don't forget the kitchen, even if guests do not eat there. Before you can gracefully stop them they may bring out their own dishes after breakfast. Some may offer to cook or to wash up. You might have a cup of coffee with guests in the kitchen even if you have served them elsewhere. So don't have a messy kitchen; it reflects on the food you serve.

We cannot emphasize cleanliness enough. Guests feel cheered by clean, sparkling surroundings. We have had people remark in almost jubilant tones, "My home isn't this clean!" People calling to make a reservation say, "We've heard you're very clean." Cleaning, unlike redecorating, costs almost nothing, but could be more important to your B&B.

Function and Comfort

Making your home functional and comfortable for B&B means that it works well and that the functions are obvious to the guests:

- The closet is empty and ready, and has enough hangers.
- The lamps are bright and placed where most likely to be used for reading and personal grooming.
- Electric cords, outlets and appliances work properly.
- Mirrors are good and the right height.
- Soap dishes, wastebaskets and towel racks are provided.
- Extra blankets, pillows, fans or heaters are visible, or guests are told where to find them.
- There are enough outlets in the bath and bedroom for use of electric shavers and hairdriers.
- There is enough hot water.
- Windows and window shades work properly.
- There is a good writing surface in the guestroom.
- There is a glass top or tray or coasters on which to place wet objects such as glasses.
- There are towel racks in both guest room and bath so guests can keep their towels separated from yours or other guests.
- There are ash trays if smoking is allowed.

Good mattresses and pillows are very important—lumpy beds and skimpy pillows can spoil the visit.

Your outside grounds should function well, too, in the sense that they be well maintained, there are chairs to sit on, a convenient parking space, and so on. When things are set up properly and function smoothly, both hosts and guests are comfortable and at ease.

Temperature and climate also affect guests' comfort. Will your room(s) be cool enough in summer? If you do not have air conditioning—and most B&Bs do not—make sure windows are screened. For really hot days, you should provide a fan.

In winter, make sure the room is warm and that there are enough blankets. We have found flannel sheets to be cozy when it is very cold. Some hosts provide electric blankets. How many regular blankets guests will use, or whether they like electric blankets, will vary. Do not make up the bed with three or four blankets on it; use one or two and let your guests choose more if they wish.

If there is no central heating—or the heating is unpredictable because your apartment landlord is stingy—quartz heaters, for focused heating, or oil-filled electric radiators are helpful. The latter, particularly, give steadier heat than electric coil heaters, and are odorless by comparison with kerosene heaters.

Safety

Safety is very important to you and your guests for obvious reasons.

- Avoid small rugs and slippery, overly waxed floors.
- Stairs, inside and outside, should have handrails and non-skid steps.
- Always have a non-skid mat in tub or shower.
- If there are icy spots on the outside walk, make sure they are sanded.
- Warn people of any problem spot, even low ceilings or low-hanging light fixtures.
- If necessary, post signs like "step down" or "low beam."
- Do not leave things around for guests to trip on.
- All potentially dangerous objects should be locked up out of reach.
- Make sure your exits are obvious, unblocked, and known to guests.
- In the city, if you live in a big apartment building, make sure your guests know elevator and stair locations.
- Smoke detectors are recommended in some places. Having a fire

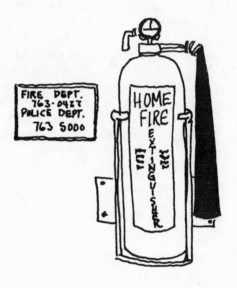

extinquisher handy, or, if the house is big, a fire ladder could be helpful.

- Leave a hall or night light on, even in a small house.
- Exterior lights should be left on as long as guests are still out.
- If you tend to have short blackouts in your area during storms, a flashlight in the guest room also can be helpful.

If you have some attractive hazard like a pond or swimming pool, be sure to make people with smaller children aware of this. If something hazardous ought to be posted, be sure it is. Talk to your insurance man when in doubt. And check your liability insurance. (See Chapter 4.)

If you are heating the guest room with a wood or kerosene heater, make sure guests understand how it functions, and make certain ventilation is provided where necessary. Stoves and heaters should be carefully maintained.

Attractiveness

Once you have made your home clean and functional for B&B, you can pursue those extras that will enhance it even more by making it as attractive as possible within whatever financial and energy limitations you have set. Remember to focus on embellishing what you already have. Enhance with little touches—little, because we strongly advise you to resist the urge to paint the whole place and repaper all the rooms before you find out if B&B is going to work for you. (Unless, of course, your game plan is to redecorate an old or new house and help pay for this from a B&B income.)

Color coordinating is a basic and inexpensive way to help make a room attractive. Your goal is to make the room feel warm and lived in, even though you may have removed the usual personal items that help create that feeling. Color helps.

When you do buy things—towels, for example—follow the sales until you find some that are the right colors. We have made towel racks of wood for each room and painted them to blend with the colors there. Using towels color-coded to each room avoids confusion if guests leave a towel behind in a shared bath. You also can line your dresser drawers with paper matching or complementing the dominant room color.

If you decide to repaint the woodwork or a night-table, color-coordinate. Don't use white enamel just because you have some left and it wears well. Many of the latex paints are very washable and yet have matte finishes, and they come in lovely colors.

Switching objects, even furniture, within or between rooms, may show both to better advantage. Perhaps the spread you are using on your bed would enhance the wallpaper in the guest room more than the spread there now? Use towels, dresser scarves and ashtrays that go best together. Not just color, but styles and textures can be coordinated to achieve a better effect.

Tone-setting

Carefully chosen and strategically placed objects enhance. A welcoming light in the window, reading material by the bedside table, a local paper, some flowers or a plant, the open guest book—all the little touches you add are part of your tone.

We found that making do with what we had and using it to the best advantage, or buying on sale only those things for which we could see an immediate use was more fun than some of our other preparations. It was a challenge, taxing our ingenuity. The special enjoyment lay in choosing and recombining various decorative objects to set our own stamp upon a room.

In the hall and in each bedroom we leave a varied assortment of books—mysteries, gothics, biographies, travel, history, and novels; and, in the bedside table drawer, crossword puzzles. We have heard guests say, "Guess what I found!" and they happily "puzzle" away.

Flowers in the room are nice but relatively expensive. We sometimes use houseplants, and, in summer, garden flowers or wild flowers like Queen Anne's Lace or Black-Eyed Susan, or berried branches from shrubs. In the fall you can make dried arrangements with milkweed, sumac pods, or the like. Since we have a greenhouse, we are able to put flowering plants in the rooms even in late winter, but just a simple green plant will add a nice touch. And, we have seen dried floral or grass arrangements in B&Bs at all seasons of the year.

Colorful or slightly different objects can enhance. For a quarter each, we bought some brightly colored art deco platters to use as dresser trays and ashtrays, and guests frequently comment on them. Old dresser scarves are much admired, as are pictures (carefully chosen) and attractive lampshades.

Some hosts offer sherry, late night coffee and cookies, disposable shower caps, toothbrushes, fresh fruit in the guest room, candy on the bed pillows, writing paper and pens and so on. If you supply these more expensive items, make sure the cost of your room reflects them.

The breakfast table is another place besides the guest room where special touches are important. We will discuss this more in Chapter 7, but keep in mind as part of your preparations that the breakfast area and the breakfast table itself also should reflect your "tone."

Your yard, if you have one, and the outside of your house, should be neat and have some colorful feature. At the least, keep the lawn cut and the garbage in an appropriate place. Plant a few eye-catching annuals, even if you do no other gardening, and do weed your flowerbeds. Of course, if you live in the city, you usually will not have to deal with outside maintenance.

Finally, get the tone you have set for your B&B into your brochure, flyer, or guidebook listing. Those things that reflect your ambience, your specialness, should come through in the language itself so that they are conveyed to potential guests.

4
Exploring Regulations

Some of your immediate questions will be concerned with the possible impact of zoning rules, health and safety laws, licensing and sales tax regulations, income tax laws and insurance coverage on your B&B plans. Don't panic and don't plunge. Take these things slowly.

First of all, you will see from a further reading of this chapter that insurance and income taxes are fairly standard for any locality. Variations in these will depend upon your volume or your business structure, not upon your location.

However, regulations concerning zoning, health codes, licensing and sales taxes can vary greatly from one area to another. Some may or may not exist in your area. Or, some may not apply, depending upon the size and set up of your B&B venture. If they are in some way applicable to your B&B, you can more easily cope with them once you have sorted them out and have the information you need to act.

Proceeding Slowly

Unless you already know how B&B in your area is affected by such regulations, you should inform yourself as much as possible before finalizing any authorization you may need.

Your first step, therefore, usually should *not* be to march into your local licensing office or zoning board and demand an instant answer. Not surprisingly, many civil servants at local, county or state levels have never heard of B&B, or do not know how or if their offices actually regulate it. In trying to answer your questions, they may confuse B&B with hotels and motels, and quote regulations which do not apply to you. Unless you have done some homework and can quote chapter and verse to them, you, as a novice yourself, will be asking rather broad questions. So do not push people into taking positions on something for which they have no precedents. Their easy out may be to say no on the principle that it is a safer answer for them than yes.

However, do not avoid dealing with these issues just because you are unsure how to approach them. We have seen the fear of being given wrong answers make beginning B&B hosts very ambivalent about asking questions. Some have simply said, "Don't ask, go ahead until someone says you cannot do it." Others feel that if they ask once and get an answer that they like, even if they still have some question about that answer, they can go ahead because they did ask. Some claim they do not even ask questions, saying they feel that since they are operating out of their own home, "government interference be damned!" While this latter attitude seems hard-nosed or even defensive, the people who voice it may in fact be operating a B&B that does not require any regulation. Some hosts in urban areas feel they are so anonymous that no one is going to know what they are doing anyway.

Do not ignore the rules. Proceed cautiously and inform yourself through as many sources as you can; then apply to the proper authority where necessary.

Informing Yourself

How do you inform yourself? In the following pages we discuss pertinent general information about each of the regulatory areas we have referred to. For specific information regarding your own area, consult local sources such as the chamber of commerce, the state department of tourism, other B&B hosts in your area, the cooperative extension service agent, RSO (reservation service organization) operators—any or all of whom may have explored similar B&B questions. Also, community colleges sometimes offer B&B seminars. (If you are considering listing with a broad-based RSO and consult them about local regulations, confirm that the advice they give you applies specifically to your locality.)

After trying such sources, if you still need further information, or think you have a problem, you might discuss things with an elected official such as a town supervisor, city councilman, or state assemblyman before you go to the relevant civil servant. Eventually, of course, having learned enough to carefully focus your questions, you may need to approach city and county clerks, state tax offices, licensing bureaus and zoning boards for further specific information or to request whatever authorization you need.

If some information you need is more generally related to the small business aspects of your B&B there are, in many cities, organizations of retired businessmen who give free consultations to small business operators. New York, for example, has the Retired Executive Volunteer Corps sponsored by the city. SCORE (Service Core of Retired Executives) is a national group sponsored by the Small Business Administration. The Internal Revenue Service offers pamphlets and some advisory information and services for small businesses.

As B&B growth continues, many RSOs are trying to deal with information-gap problems. There are almost no organizations of hosts doing so. The need is great for individual B&B operators to form their own state-wide organizations and share information and experiences. While it is likely that we will see this happening during the next few years, this of course offers you no immediate help.

Meantime, therefore, we remind you that while it may be tedious to establish which regulations apply to your B&B—indeed, you may explore something for some months and then find that it does not apply—if your volume of business is large enough, then some things become obligatory. So explore regulations, keeping in mind the size of your home, the frequency with which you have guests, whether you are serving meals other than breakfast, and so on. It won't really be that hard to do, and once you've done it, you're "on your way."

Zoning

Zoning restrictions may or may not exist where you are. Some localities do not have any; some do not apply to B&Bs; some are strict and must be conformed with, or you must get a variance.

It has generally been the case that if you do not hang out a shingle (i.e., look commercial in a residential neighborhood), or create parking, traffic or noise problems for your neighbors, you are less likely to have problems with zoning laws. Make sure that the way you operate your B&B will not upset your neighbors. You should not impose upon them. Our own experience in a small town has included asking our neighbors to take in our overflow guests. It has worked out well for all of us. Letting your neighbors know what you are doing—explaining B&B to them—might be a help. Or, asking interested neighbors to join a small B&B network, with you doing the major effort might also make the neighborhood more at ease with the B&B concept. Indeed, if you are in an area where you need to get a zoning variance, having the support of neighbors and local businesses—who might use your services for their customers—could be helpful in getting the board to approve your application.

In the event that someone does complain, laws which were set up to exclude inns, hotels, motels, rooming houses or other businesses from a residential neighborhood may be cited. These kinds of businesses will be compared to B&B, but they are not the same thing. It would be up to you to make the distinction clear to the zoning board. You might also need to explain that your guests are not a permanent rental (i.e., tenant) or a sublet, and that you are not running a boarding house.

Note also that zoning usually allows for small businesses customarily done in the home, such as those of hairdressers, doctors, lawyers, accountants, caterers and music teachers. You should demonstrate that you, also, are running a home-based business. You also might indicate that B&B is not causing your home to deteriorate, but that you are keeping it spiffier, inside and out, since you started B&B.

The *New York Times Business Section* of September 11, 1983, reported a case in Westchester County, New York, in which a B&B host challenged her zoning board. She pointed out that her B&B guest home—which "now has fewer visitors than it did during the 90 years when it contained offices for three generations of doctors"—was definable as a "customary home occupation" which "had no signs, no goods on display, no non-residential purposes." Demonstrating how the B&B concept conformed to the existing zoning law, she won her case.

It is unlikely that you will find yourself challenged in such a way, but this case should be noted as an example of an informed B&B host who worked within existing laws, made the community more familiar with B&B, and gained acceptance from the authorities.

Licensing

Licensing may vary from state to state, or county to county. Whether you need any licenses probably depends on the number of rooms, the volume of business you do, and whether or not you are serving meals other than breakfast. In some states, if you are using only one or two rooms, or using more rooms but not averaging many persons daily, then you do not need a license. Of course, if you are serving meals, then you may need one or more licenses connected with food-handling and service. Or, if you sell drinks to guests, rather than just giving complimentary drinks or wine, you need a liquor license. Find out what other B&Bs and RSOs are doing in your area.

Sales Tax

At this writing, it is not mandatory in many states that sales tax be collected for B&B accommodations in one's own home. It should be fairly simple to establish whether or not your state requires that you collect sales tax on your B&B earnings. However, before we finally resolved this question for our B&B, we got two different answers from two different state offices. Therefore, we suggest you get your answer, preferably in writing, from your state department of taxation and finance. Do not ignore this matter. It is not worth attracting the negative attention of the state tax office. If you should have been collecting the tax, you will pay assessments and penalties for every month you waited.

Sales tax is not difficult to collect. Find out exactly what percentage it is, and automatically add it on as you bill your guests. Get a sales tax number from your county clerk or the state. The clerk will give you a payment schedule as well. If you collect only a minimal amount of sales tax because your volume of business is low, you may have to pay it only once a year.

Some states may have business taxes. If your B&B is in a large city, there may be a municipal tax on room rentals, possibly related to length of stay. Because you are a private individual taking occasional paying guests into your own home, you are not likely to be subject to taxes which are applicable to hotels and motels, but you should inform yourself and act accordingly.

Health and Sanitary Codes

If you have one or two rooms and are serving breakfast only, you probably are not subject to any state health department regulation. However, if you are serving other meals there could be sanitary and health codes which apply. These could call for expensive changes in your kitchen, involving commercial equipment, monitoring of dishwashing temperatures, and food-handling rules. Asking guests to eat with the family once in a while, if the mood strikes you, is not "serving meals." But unless you are intending to run a restaurant on your premises, do be careful to avoid any suggestion that you are regularly serving meals for money. In several states the health department has definitively ruled that B&Bers do not come under the state restaurant code. Find out the regulations for your area.

Insurance

You should ask your insurance agent in writing and get a definitive answer in writing as to whether your homeowner's policy as it is now written covers you for the various contingencies—fire, theft, liability—that could arise while you have B&B guests in your home.

This is a new area for insurance agents. They may not understand B&B, or they may give you a qualified answer such as that your usual homeowner's liability probably covers you if you have only two guests or an "occasional overnight paying guest." If you are a small B&B taking in only a very limited number of guests, you may be covered. If, however, you are taking in guests on a high volume basis and more than two at one time, it might be wise to buy extra insurance coverage.

You may also want to double-check your automobile liability coverage if you are taking guests to and from airports and train stations. And, with reference to fire insurance, make sure that you have done whatever your locality might require (e.g., smoke detectors, fire extinguishers) for you to be in compliance with any applicable fire laws.

Make sure any additional coverage you buy is suitable—that it gives fire and theft as well as liability coverage. If your present broker cannot give you this, go to a company that can give you a "commercial package" covering these items.

Some companies already are writing policies for groups of B&B hosts. If there are enough of you in your area, your broker might be able to get group coverage, and of course group premiums will be less expensive. You also can get group coverage by joining an RSO (reservation service organization) or listing in a guide that offers it to their members. Group policies may cover only additional liability, not fire and theft. Check this out before you buy. Premiums vary from $25-$100 annually, so shop around. (See Part VI: Resources.)

Both B&B hosts and RSO groups are raising the issue of insurance coverage with state insurance offices and individual insurance brokers in an effort to develop cheaper and better coverage for B&B hosts. For now, however, you must work with what is currently available.

Income Tax

The specific relevance to you of the income tax discussion that follows will vary with your individual situation. Also, remember that tax laws are constantly reviewed and changed. For these reasons, we suggest you seek competent tax counsel.

B&B income usually is subject to federal income and Social Security taxes. However, if you are a taxpayer who rents your own home for less than fifteen days a year, then you do not need to report the B&B income. Rental income after the fourteenth day is taxable, and you can take deductions and depreciation allowances against it. If your B&B income is very small, you might want to call it hobby income and avoid Social Security taxes. However, if you do this you cannot qualify as a business and may lose other tax advantages. And, if you do not turn a profit in at least two of five years hosting B&B, then, the IRS may look upon this as hobby income rather than business income.

Assess beforehand the potential impact of B&B income and outgo on your tax situation. What you learn may influence how you structure your B&B operation. Consult an accountant or talk to the IRS. The IRS has offices in many cities and a toll-free number in every telephone directory. While the IRS may not know what a B&B is, you can present them with details regarding your own small business situation.

When filling out your tax return for B&B, if you have some taxable income from other sources as well you will file the usual Form 1040, plus Schedule C. If you net over $400 in B&B income, you also will file Form 1040 S.E. (Self-Employed). The latter is used for Social Security taxation of that part of your income not subject to withholding.

If you net over $100 quarterly or $500 annually with B&B, then—assuming this income is not covered, or not enough of it is covered by withholding—you must pay estimated taxes quarterly using Form 1040 S.E. Make sure Social Security taxes are included in your payment.

If you will be due a tax refund at the end of the year, or will need to pay less than $500 annually, then you need not pay estimated taxes. Form 1040, Schedule C, and Form 1040 S.E. will suffice.

In using Schedule C, you are treating your B&B income as *earned* income. That is, you do more than just rent your house to receive this income (e.g., you prepare food, you regularly clean up after guests and do their laundry, you work to publicize your B&B, and so on). It is your home-based business. Thus, most accountants interpret B&B income as earned income. However, there is another possible interpretation that could and sometimes probably is used. This interpretation sees B&B income as straight rental income, which therefore is reported on Schedule E rather than Schedule C. Earned income is subject to Social Security taxes and rental income is not. Also, any Keogh deduction applies to Schedule C income but not Schedule E income. This might make some difference to you, depending on your personal circumstances. Again, we urge you to seek professional tax counsel to clarify such things for you, especially the first year you do B&B.

Keep records of expenses in order to back up your deductions. Some of these are one-time only. Examples are deductions for painting and wallpapering done in preparation for B&B. You must take such deductions for the first year that you incur the expense.

Other deductions are depreciated over a period of time and are called capital expenses. They are related to the useful life of specific objects such as furniture, towels, sheets, and other things used over several years. Some percentage of their value is deductible each year. That portion of the house itself which is being used for B&B also can be depreciated. For example, if two rooms in a nine-room house are set aside for paying guests, then 22% of the original purchase price plus improvements, less the cost of the land, can be depreciated. Some hosts use this formula to depreciate the kitchen, bathroom, and living room as well for that period of time guests are using or actually being served in them.

Examples of normal, annually recurring deductions for B&B would include: chamber of commerce dues; subscriptions to B&B publications; the price of this book; commissions or fees paid to RSOs or to be listed in guidebooks and the cost of brochure printing. Also, operating expenses such as utilities, fuel, food, maintenance and laundry, but only those portions which directly relate to your B&B, are deductible. The *IRS Tax Guide for Small Businesses* lists both kinds of deductions. Accountants suggest some IRS booklets: #334, #17, and #583 as being helpful to small businesses and B&B'ers. Even if you are accustomed to doing your own taxes and feel quite confident about dealing with B&B income, we again suggest in your first year to have an accountant double-check your returns.

Special Tax Advantages

If you are a senior citizen with low Social Security or other qualifying pension, there is a tax credit for the elderly which you might be able to utilize. Also, anyone who already has an individual IRA may, as a result of having a B&B or other business, open in addition a self-employed retirement plan (Keogh or SEP) and deposit in it up to 20% of their net self-employment income, thereby reducing their tax bill. Consult your lawyer and accountant about these special plans.

Historic Preservation Tax Credits

Tax credits and low-cost mortgages may be had if a house has special distinction as being historic or is in an historic district and is certified as such by the Department of Interior. A series of tax law revisions—the Tax Reform Act of 1976; the Revenue Act of 1976; the Tax Treatment Extension Act of 1980; the Economic Recovery Tax Act of 1981, and the Tax Reform Act of 1984—taken together have various provisions, including investment tax credits, regarding such houses or buildings. Look into this if you think you might be eligible.

To qualify for tax credits for restoration you must be using the building for commercial purposes, such as for example, B&B. If the house or building is fifty years old or older, the tax credit can be as high as 25%. If the house is 30-40 years old, the credit may be 15% to 20%.

The Department of Interior in Washington, D.C., can send you a booklet specifying exactly the kind of restoration that qualifies. Their regional offices also can help. (See Part VI: Resources.)

Each state has state historic preservation officers who will be able to tell you whether your district is historic and whether your home might qualify to be on the National Register of Historic Places.

Call the preservation officer in your state capital and discuss your individual situation. He or she can give you application forms for the certification procedure and also information about tax credits available for such restorations. Getting a house nominated and certified on the Register is harder than obtaining historic district designation.

If your house is not very old, or historic, or you do not intend the kind of restoration required by the Department of Interior, you still may qualify for some tax relief. Under some of the tax acts noted previously rehabilitating under-utilized or abandoned buildings for new uses may also provide tax credits of 15% to 25%. The tax person in your state preservation office will know something

about this. So will the IRS or your accountant. Ask one of these sources to explore this with you.

In certain cases, for these kinds of houses or buildings HUD might give low-cost mortgages. Some states and municipalities will give other tax breaks. If you own or are thinking of buying such a house or building to restore or renovate, explore these possibilities. It could result in substantial savings to you.

PART III
Getting Underway

5

Systematizing Your B&B

Trying to do even a medium-volume business without efficient operating systems could become a headache, especially if you are not a full-time host. There are things that must be done regularly and some of them are pretty prosaic. Try to maximize the fun parts and cut the tedium of the less-glamorous ones by being well-organized. Know what you have to do and when. Do as much beforehand as you can. Follow the systems and check-lists suggested in this chapter to keep things running smoothly so you can enjoy the weekend.

Scheduling and Reservations

This is a telephone-oriented, last-minute-planning world we live in: while some guests will write to you, many more will call.

Keep by your telephone a large notebook or calendar. Circle dates and write in names and addresses as soon as you receive a call or letter. When a deposit arrives, write "DEP" or some such abbreviation after the name so that you know the reservation is solid. If there is time you may wish to write back and confirm. Unless our guests specifically ask us to do this, we do not bother. Do expect people to change travel plans and dates, so make calendar notations in pencil, not ink.

Keep track of reservations in an organized way, or you may wind up with two bookings for one room on the same day. At the last minute you will have to cancel or get a back-up booking for one of your guest parties. Conversely, you might turn someone away because you think a date is filled and then, too late, find out your mistake. Do not think that this cannot happen to you. It can and will during a busy season, unless you have your reservation schedule well in hand.

Some guests do write or call well in advance, and you can send them back a brochure—a highly recommended procedure. They then have both a chance to look over exactly what you are offering and time to send a deposit. Usually you can assume that reservations scheduled early and accompanied by deposits are firm, although sometimes people do get sick or change plans for other reasons.

Many of your guests will phone requests for rooms too late for a deposit to reach you before they arrive. Tell such callers that you usually require a deposit, and that you are reluctant to confirm and are doing so only out of kindness; that if they do not show up and you have turned someone else away, you will lose money because of them. Tell them that if they are not there by a specific time, and have not phoned to reconfirm, you will rent the room to someone else.

If guests in residence make a date to return in a few weeks, ask them for a deposit, too. Many people, full of enthusiasm for your B&B, tell you that they will be back. Sooner or later most of them probably will be, but it could be weeks, months, or next year before this happens. Don't forego the deposit just because you are familiar with someone. They are also feeling familiar with you and may expect you to make an exception for them. Stick to your policy, even with new-found friends.

Remember to put your own social engagements on the calendar—especially things like weddings or graduations which have absolutely fixed dates—otherwise you may unwittingly accept a reservation for a date when you want to be elsewhere. You then will have to call back (an unnecessary expenditure) or not go to the wedding, or arrange for someone else to be there to greet your guests and shift them to another accommodation. Such confusion won't help with return business or recommendations.

If you cannot be there to answer your phone during the day, your guide listings or your brochure or business card should note evening hours during which to call. If you have an answering machine, you can put on your tape a backup number (perhaps a neighbor's or relative's) or tell callers to leave their name, address and reservation date and you will confirm by return mail. We invested in a machine and found that it soon paid for itself in reservations we might otherwise have missed.

Setting House Rules

Your B&B policies should be conveyed to guests via house rules and your brochures or advertising. House rules are your way of defining your policies and then managing your B&B according to them. They should embody what is comfortable and efficient for you, as well as be a guide for the guest. These policies might include:

- Where you allow smoking and drinking.
- Whether and times guests may use the living room, second bath, kitchen, refrigerator, TV, pool, picnic table, balcony, patio, yard, iron, clothesline, laundry.
- Where guests can walk and feed pets (not in the room).
- Time you will lock up, and where guests get a key if they will be in after that hour.
- Instructions about towel racks and wet clothes and towels.
- Instructions about telephone usage—location of phone, times to use, payment for long distance.
- Availability of extra blankets and pillows, and location of same.
- Check-in and check-out time; allowing luggage to be left after that.
- Minimum stay policy (e.g., at least two days) if you have one.
- Cautions about wooden furniture, wet cups and glasses.

- Payment times, and whether you take checks or credit cards or cash only.
- Hours between which breakfast is served; type of breakfast served.
- Things particular to your house (e.g., jiggle toilet handle, hard faucet, faucet turns wrong way, location of things, etc.).
- Fire instructions, stairways, etc. if not apparent.
- Any services, tours, etc. you offer or sell.
- If tea or coffee is available in guest room or kitchen during the day or evening, or drinks in the living room or on the patio.
- If a key deposit is required.

If you put all your house rules on one list and posted them in the guest room, it would overwhelm guests. Besides, they should know some policies *before* booking with you. Use the telephone or better yet, your brochure, to advise guests for example, if you: do not allow smoking; take cash only; allow pets; have pets in residence (some guests may be allergic to them); do not allow children under a certain age.

Check-in and check-out times, besides being noted in the brochure, can be posted on the back of the guest room door along with fire-exit notes. Other rules can be indicated when guests arrive. Show them the house, where they can sit, lounge, or walk their pets. Breakfast rules if you have them, can be noted on your breakfast check sheet.

Locations of light switches that are hard to find can be tacked on the outside of bedroom and bathroom doors. If you let guests use your refrigerator, barbecue, picnic table, or the kitchen, post your clean-up rules in the area. The same applies if you want each guest to clean the tub after using. Post instructions prominently in the bathroom. In the city, rules clarifying house switchboard, doormen and announcing systems can be posted in the guest room.

Your phone rules should be clearly stated and tacked over or near the telephone. Remind guests that they can charge long distance calls to their home phone or credit card. Rule out on a pad a record of calls and leave it, and pencils, by the telephone for guests to note time called, number called, length of call and charges, which they can get from the operator immediately after making the call. (In some areas you may have to ask your operator in advance to time calls; check this out.) Use this log yourself to get information from the operator if necessary. You may also use this phone record pad to take messages for guests.

Some rules which are more instructional—such as not putting wet glasses on the furniture—can be part of a house-rules or "Dear Guest" letter or a notice put on the desk in the guest room. Head it with a large "WELCOME" and combine some hospitable things (e.g., "There is a pot of coffee on the stove." "There are extra blankets in the hall closet." "Ask, if you want anything.") with admonitions such as "Don't hang wet towels on the backs of varnished chairs." Keep a light touch, so that no one feels you are hassling them. Some rules should be repeated in several places to make sure that they are absolutely clear.

Providing Information

Guests may expect information from you as the "resident expert." You of course do not have to be an expert, but it is a nice touch if you can provide them with local information when they need it.

An easy and helpful thing to have is a sheet with telephone numbers, and maybe addresses, and hours available, for the following:

- Local churches and synagogues.
- Doctor, dentist, pediatrician, veterinarian, baby sitter.
- Bookstores, health food stores, notions stores, hair dresser, gas station, mechanic, travel agent.
- Fire, police, poison control, rescue squad, ambulance.
- Restaurants, movies, museums, concert halls, theatres.
- Places for swimming, golf, tennis, skiing, horseback riding, bicycle rental.

If you do make recommendations, know who or what you are recommending. If you do not know from your own personal experience, find out what you can from others. For example, if you do not have a pet, ask someone who does about local veterinarians. If you recommend a local restaurant, know their approximate price range, the kind of food they serve, and whether reservations are necessary. Try to have sample menus on hand so people can decide for themselves. Know the admission rules and hours for things like tennis courts, nature preserves, golf courses and so on.

Many of the more commercial attractions such as museums or historic houses will have brochures available. Go to them, or to the local chamber of commerce or, in larger cities, the tourist information bureau, and get brochures to leave in your guest rooms for visitors to browse through when planning their next day's outing. Guests appreciate these and usually take some, so be sure to replace them regularly.

We always have the local paper handy for arriving guests. They can check out upcoming events, activity calendars, auction advertisements and real estate listings. Guests all seem to enjoy reading the paper and often plan their activities around something noted there.

Even though the big cities are likely to have printed, detailed guides, there are always things going on that are not well-publicized. For example, the sailboat races on the Hudson River in New York City every October for the Mayor's Cup would be more interesting to many people than is the marathon that same month, but comparatively few people know about it. Try to be informed about interesting or less publicized events. The local, authentic and, to them, unusual events can be the high spot of guests' weekends.

Bone up on travel directions. Be able to tell guests how to get around your area either via the fastest or the most scenic way, whichever they desire. In both hamlets and cities, there may be interesting walks, bike trails, buildings and the like which you might mention. And know how long it will take them to get where they want to go.

Local maps usually are available free from real estate brokers, insurance agents and merchants who have these imprinted with their addresses as advertising. Try to get a supply of these for your guests. Have a larger area map by your telephone. Guests often call to get directions from an interstate highway or parkway. Be able to tell them where to exit and which roads to take after that. They may count on you to get them to your home.

In the big cities, know parking regulations, parking garage locations and which streets are one-way in which direction near you. Bus and subway maps usually are available from the metropolitan transportation group in your city. Know the numbers to call for train and bus schedule information.

ENTERTAINMENT FOR JUNE — AUGUST
6/12 THEATRE FESTIVAL
6/26 GARDEN SHOW
7/1 POP CONCERT
7/4 INDEPENDENCE DAY GALA
7/19 FOUNDER'S DAY
7/30 HORSE RACES
8/6 ARTS & CRAFTS SHOW
8/28 LAST BASH BEFORE SCHOOL DANCE

PETE SEEGER
SINGS FOR THE RIVER PEOPLE

OUTDOOR CONCERT
6:30 PM
FRIDAY, AUGUST 23
BOLLFIELD OFF BOLL AVE
ADULTS 4.00 CHILD 1.00
REFRESHMENTS SOLD

Breakfast Check Sheet

When guests arrive you may not always remember to check their breakfast preferences, as you are busy registering them and answering their questions. Rather than having breakfast too early or fixing something they do not want, check things out the night before. If, for example, you forgot to check before the guests went off to supper and you now want to go to bed, leave the breakfast checksheet by the front door: one for each guest. The check sheet can look something like this:

WE SERVE BREAKFAST BETWEEN 7:30 AND 10:00 AM
WHEN DURING THAT TIME WOULD YOU LIKE BREAKFAST?
PLEASE CHECK YOUR PREFERENCE FOR:

Coffee	English Muffins	Orange Juice
Tea	Donuts	V8 Juice
Milk	Toast	Tomato Juice
Herbal Tea		

If you leave breakfast out for guests to serve themselves, you do not need to establish an exact time for breakfast, but you still should specify within what time period breakfast is available so that the rest of your morning is free.

If you are cooking things you should clear it with guests in case there is anything they cannot eat. Some may have allergies or be on a low sodium diet.

Guest Satisfaction Check Sheet

Some B&B hosts leave check sheets in the guest rooms so that guests can note their satisfactions and dissatisfactions. Some reservation service organizations (RSOs) ask their affiliated B&B hosts to have these available so that the RSO can rate the individual host. We have chosen not to have such a check list in our rooms—it seems so impersonal in an old and homey house.

We have found that after you have been a host for a bit, and are used to "good reviews," your guest barometer will let you know if someone seems a bit reserved or unhappy. In that case, ask the guest very directly if everything is all right. If there is a problem, deal with it, don't ignore it.

If you do want to have a guest satisfaction sheet, note the sample one below and adapt it to your needs.

Rating	Guest room	Bath	Breakfast	Host	Other
Very Satisfactory					
Satisfactory					
Unsatisfactory					
Very Poor					

Please give details for your ratings: e.g., host very accommodating or bath not clean, and so on.

Housekeeping

Housekeeping will seem a less interesting part of B&B, but it has to be done, and probably by you. Most B&Bs do not have cleaning service.

Do not put off cleaning your guest rooms. Last-minute preparations, done in haste, do not give arriving guests the impression of a well-run B&B. The bulk of your preparation should be done at a leisurely pace during the course of the week, since you can almost always count on weekends being busier than midweek. We clean the guest room and bath, strip and remake beds and replace towels in several sessions, and as soon as possible after guests have left.

If you wish, some chores such as last-minute dusting can be done closer to the time when guests arrive. You also may want to save general cleaning of the rest of the house or apartment until then. But keep in mind that you may have "drop-ins" from local people, who want to look over your B&B before they plan accommodations for guests to their wedding or party. And, if you are in the Yellow Pages or a guidebook, you may get last-minute calls. So if you are doing a high volume business, things must be kept neat, especially during your busy season.

If you have pets, keep them out of the guest rooms, as they may sleep on furniture and leave their fur about. During summer, there can be a flea problem, so make these rooms off-limits to pets.

Once you have guests in residence, you should change their sheets every two to three days; certainly no longer than a weekend. Some hosts give clean towels every day, some every other day. If you have a pool, they will need more towels more often. Plan your sheet and towel changes to take place when guests are not around.

Most guests want to make their own beds. They take over their room as their own for the course of the weekend. If it makes you more comfortable, ask when guests arrive if they want you to make their bed. They usually will say no. We leave it to them and do not mention it one way or the other. Some larger B&Bs do have cleaning service and change linens daily, especially in heavy tourist areas where the host has too many rooms and too many guests at one time to handle everything alone.

If you have more than one set of guests at a time, it is a good idea to check the bathroom at least once a day to make sure that each has left it clean for the other party. Remind guests not to leave their towels in a shared bath. Even if you have posted instructions telling them to clean up after themselves, check anyway. This room should look exceptionally clean at all times. Check the tub, shower, sink and toilet at intervals during a busy weekend. Make sure that extra tissue, toilet paper and soap are always there and visible.

We place individual soap dishes in each room, color-coded, so each guest can keep track of their own soap. Some hosts use the same bar of soap for the same room until it is used up; some cut larger bars of soap into small pieces so that only one guest uses the soap; some hosts buy the kinds of individually wrapped soaps you see in hotels and motels and some use liquid soap dispensers. Make the choice that best fits your style of B&B.

After guests have left, immediately check their rooms to see if they have forgotten anything or if they have left anything wet lying about. Many people nowadays are not used to varnished or waxed or stained wooden furniture. They think that all surfaces are plastic laminate and tolerate wet towels and glasses. It is just a sign of the times, but you must protect older furniture from this.

Also check for breakage after they leave. We have never had a breakage problem, but we always check, as a matter of course, for insurance purposes.

Supply Inventory Check List

Always know your supply inventory. Do not be caught without soap, toilet paper, orange juice, or other basics. Be sure that everything you need is on hand. The kinds of furnishings and supplies you will need are listed below.

2 sets of sheets and pillow cases
   for each bed
2 sets of towels and washclothes
   for each guest
bathmats
mattress pads
pillows, including extras
quilts, blankets, sheet blankets
dresser scarves
table cloths or mats

bed or beds
side table or stand
dresser
chair or chairs
lamps
rugs

vacuum cleaner
dust mop or broom
disinfectant spray
cleansers
furniture oil
dust cloths
vacuum cleaner bags

ash trays
soap dishes
soap
towel racks
hangers
wastebaskets
vases
paper cups
metal or ceramic or
   glass trays
light bulbs
tissue and toilet
   paper

and, possibly
clothes washer and
   dryer
fan
heater
answering machine
smoke detector
luggage rack
fire extinguisher
radio or TV
long mirror
band-aids
sewing kit

guest book
envelopes
rubber stamp
ink pad
large pad of unlined paper
record book or ledger
receipts book
tourist brochures

breakfast dishes	several kinds of juice
flatware	bread or muffins
juice glasses	coffee
coffee and teapots	tea
cream pitcher	jam
sugar bowl	butter
butter dish	sugar
	milk or cream

Remember our emphasis on planning ahead and buying at sales. If your volume warrants it, you can save on such things as small individually wrapped soaps, plastic cups, disposable bath mats, towels, sheets and other items by purchasing in quantity from supply houses specializing in these. Soon after you list in a guide you will probably get catalogs from such places, or your RSO can give you names of some. In larger cities, hotel and restaurant supply houses, which carry such items, are listed in the Yellow Pages.

Cleaning

Systematize cleaning and do it methodically so it will not seem tedious. Cut it down to size by making it a series of tasks which you do and then check off. Make a game of it, get it over with, then step back and admire the nice room at your leisure. Taking pleasure in the end product helps get the work done.

If possible, always have a towel and sheet change on hand so you can put out new towels and make the beds at the time you strip them, rather than waiting to get the laundry done. Otherwise, to keep the room looking presentable, you may have to make up the bed with the spread on it, then remake it when you get the laundry back.

It saves on laundry bills if you can do the sheets and towels when you have other things to wash as well, so don't do your B&B laundry at separate times from your other household laundry if you can help it. But do keep B&B laundry charges as separate as possible for tax purposes.

We divide our work into three different short sessions, which helps get through repetitious cleaning procedures during a busy season. We sometimes reverse steps 2 and 3 depending on how much laundry we have and whether other guests are coming immediately.

Step 1. Strip linens, put into bag.

Replace sheets and towels (remake bed).

Empty trash, ashtrays, old flowers, etc. into one plastic wastebasket.

Step 2. Use disinfectant spray on toilets and washbowls.

Dust floors, windowsills, furniture, bedsteads, lamps.

Check corners, including ceilings, for cobwebs.

Vacuum rugs, and other areas if necessary.

Scrub bowl and toilet with disinfectant, clean all mirrors, soap dishes and ashtrays.

Replace soap, paper cups, toilet paper, tissue and bouquets if applicable.

Vacuum or wipe down rugs and stairs leading to guest rooms so nothing tracks into your clean room.

Step 3. Do laundry and replace it in your storage area, with sheets-and towels for each room stacked together for quick retrieval.

Step 4. Every once in a while, as needed, vacuum or air mattress; damp-mop floors; wash quilts and bedspreads; clean and polish furniture.

Record-keeping

You must keep systematic records, mostly because of sales and income tax. If you want your deductions, you must prove income and expenditures.

It helps record-keeping to get a B&B business checking account and pay for most things through that. Many expenditures will be too small to pay by check, however, so you will need a ledger or running account and a petty cash box. Everything you bring in, plus sales tax, is deposited in the account. Everything you spend on B&B, even indirectly, is via check or petty cash. Get dated receipts with your name and the item and any sales tax clearly stated, for everything you buy.

The usual exception to this procedure is food costs. It is hard to separate B&B expenditures for things like bread, butter, and

orange juice—things which you, also, eat—from your own expenditures. Here the guest book is a great help because it proves your annual volume. Use it to calculate the number of guests times so much coffee, tea, bread, cream, butter, jelly, fruit, or whatever else you served. Estimate what an average breakfast costs you, including gas and electric, and multiply that by the number of individual guests you have served annually to get your breakfast costs.

The guestbook is also helpful in reminding you of seasonal changes and tempos which affect your expenditures or your time schedule.

Developing a Backup Network

Having a backup B&B network can be a godsend in times of heavy demand. It allows you extra flexibility and mitigates over-booking crises. Couples often travel together, and there have been times when we have had only one room available where two were needed. Being able to place the second couple with a nearby neighbor down the street or across the green was a ready solution. They could go to their auction or concert or real estate broker, have supper together, and not have their weekend plans impeded. Usually we arrange for them to have breakfast together at one house or the other. Without this backup network, we would have turned away weekend rentals. And, it gave our neighbors unexpected income.

Sometimes during a very busy weekend—major holidays or fall foliage season, for instance—travelers will phone late at night. They have been looking for several hours, and are desperate for a room. They call from a local restaurant, bar or general store, having heard that we "put people up." (If we have any questions, we ask the storekeeper or restaurant owner if they look okay before we agree to try to find a place for them.) If we cannot take them in because we are booked, our neighbors probably can, so we call around. Guests are grateful when you do them such a favor, and it has meant repeat business for us. In the city, when there is a snowstorm and traffic is tied up, many commuters would rather stay in town, and the same heavy-demand situation applies. Then a neighbor's apartment might come in handy.

There may be times when a favorite guest wants to book with you but you want to be on vacation, or you may actually—for a very important reason only—have to cancel a reservation already made. By staying with a neighbor, your guests can still be in the same general location. If you are a working host and something comes up at the office so that you cannot be home at exactly the time you promised, someone in your backup network could welcome your guest for you and get them settled in.

Developing such a backup network is a slow process but not a hard one. Keep asking likely people whose homes you think are appropriate for B&B and whom you think might welcome the guests and the income. Some, after asking a few questions, will say no or yes right away. Others will think about it or try it once before becoming a part of your list of alternatives. Those who have tried B&B hosting with us, seem to have enjoyed it and found it an easy way to make money, because we had already done the work of advertising and locating the guest.

We have extended our backup network by talking to other B&B hosts in other parts of our county and visiting their homes to see what they are like. Often, people call us and want a specific location in the county and we are able to send them along to another B&B closer to their goal. In turn, these B&B hosts have sent guests to us on particularly busy weekends.

A backup system is certainly not your first focus but it will help you be more systematic about dealing with extra guests. Develop it at your leisure, not in your prime time, and sooner or later it will provide solutions to booking problems.

6
Hosting

There is general agreement amongst B&B writers that B&B guests are the *crème de la crème* of the traveling public. Hosts say that they have never had anything stolen, and that their guests are polite, interesting and considerate people. We certainly can confirm this from our own experience. In spite of such reassurances, you, as a new host, may have some qualms about letting strangers into your home. A special concern will be whether, or how much, guests should be screened.

Screening

There are various degrees of screening. Some hosts feel that the kind of person who wants to stay in a B&B home is usually very reliable, and that by talking to them over the telephone, even for a few minutes, they can judge if this is the kind of guest they want. At the other extreme, some hosts want guests to be thoroughly screened by a reservation service organization (RSO) before actually taking their reservation.

The degree to which you feel the need to screen people will depend partly upon your own personal circumstances. For instance, if you are a woman hosting alone, or if your home is full of valuable antiques, you may want a more rigorous guest-screening than might another host. In that case, you definitely should consider joining an RSO that can do screening for you. Do keep in mind, though, that there are a number of ways that you, the host, can screen guests as part of the process of taking reservations and registering them.

You will automatically have done some screening through your brochure or guidebook listing by indicating whether you allow social drinking, smoking, children, pets, hunters, and so on. Each of these limitations screens your potential guest population.

Screening continues when the guest writes or calls you. Make some judgments from your telephone conversation. Be sure to ask how they heard of you. It may be a referral from a friend or previous guest. Get into conversation; describe your home; ask them if they want double or single beds, their arrival time, what route they are taking. You will feel something about them as they answer your questions or react to your information. If you do not like the sound of the person calling, you will tell them that you are booked, and end it.

Rejecting guests during a phone call does not necessarily mean they sound unpleasant or unreliable. It may be that you do not think B&B is for them. They may sound hesitant, have called B&B only because the motels are full, and you can tell from their voice that they are reluctant to stay in a private home. You may decide that, for your mutual comfort, it is better to tell them you are booked. We learned our first lesson about this late one evening when we had a desperate call from a local resident who had four moving men hanging about his living room because their truck had stuck in his yard. After much conversation, with his vouching personally for them, we agreed to take them in, much to the relief of the caller. A few minutes later he called back with apologies to say that the men would be embarrassed to go into a private home where they didn't know anyone, and thanks but they would sleep in their truck.

Whether people call or write, you will have—because you should always ask for it—their names and addresses. You will also ask for a deposit, and mail them a brochure if time allows. Some hosts ask for a business address as well. These procedures establish where guests live and work.

Some hosts do not put their address on their brochure or guidebook listing, but give only a box number and telephone number. They send their address and directions to their home only when they confirm the reservation.

When guests arrive, they must sign their name and address in the guest book. Some hosts ask for automobile license number, telephone and business address, or for some kind of ID, such as a driver's license or credit card. This is a further screening process. And, during this arrival time you will have been sizing up your guests and deciding whether or not you want to caution them about the cat, offer them coffee, and especially, give them your house key.

Most hosts do give their house or apartment keys to their guests. We do so to avoid staying up to let in late returnees. Many hosts do so because they are away at work during the day and want their guests to have access to the home. Some hosts require a stiff deposit if they give out a key. Some have two locks and only give out the key for one. Some, as we do, simply have extra keys on hand. Only twice has someone gone off with our key, and one of them mailed it back with apologies.

If for some reason you do not want to give out a key, set a limit to the time you will stay up and let people in. Those hosts who work and do not want to give guests a key will find it awkward trying to be present whenever guests are in residence. In such cases it might be better to work through an RSO which will screen for you; then you will feel free to give out keys, and not be inconvenienced. Do keep in mind that thousands of hosts list themselves in regional or national guidebooks, available in any book store or library, and describe their antique-filled houses. They are open to the passing traveler as well as the one who phones or writes ahead. Yet B&B guests continue to have good records. You will have to decide what degree of screening makes you comfortable, and go with that.

Arrival Time

If you are home to greet guests personally, do it warmly with a smile and a friendly hello. Make them feel welcome. Some may be staying in B&B by chance and even those familiar with B&B may feel some reserve upon first coming into your home. Break the ice for both of you by encouraging guests to talk about themselves. Ask: "Did you have a good drive?" "Did you have any trouble finding us?" "Was it bad driving in this weather?"

The guest book also is an icebreaker. Have guests sign in as soon as possible. It gives them something "official" to do. And if you want payment on arrival, collect it gracefully as a part of registration.

Begin at once to orient them as to their room, the location of the bath, which parts of the house or apartment they can use, where they will eat breakfast, how to turn on the fan or heater, or how to open a tricky window. Some guests will be shy, and tippy-toe around, whispering, until they understand where their "turf" is in your home. Then they loosen up and relax. Do keep in mind that when people have been driving for a long time, the first thing they may want, before making scintillating conversation with you, the gracious host, is to use the bathroom. So make arriving a quick and easy process.

Ask if there is anything special they need to know because of their particular reason for being in the area. Most guests have an agenda for their stay and want to make sure they see or do certain things. And they almost always want to know where can they eat; how do they get to such and such a place and how long will it take; is it okay to park where they are; and how do they get in if they come back late? After a few visits, greeting guests will become easy for you, and you will begin to anticipate their questions.

During arrival, or in the course of the weekend, introduce to them your family, friends, children and other guests as they meet. There should be no air of having anonymous persons wandering about. But do keep children, pets, and friends out of guest rooms. Allow guests their privacy.

If you work or are renting out your apartment while you are away, you probably will not be there to greet your guests. In that case, you will have to communicate with them in writing. Use the information provided in chapters 5, 6, and 7 to develop rules and instructions to guide your guests in using your home on their own when you are not there. You might want to write a long and chatty "guestletter" covering what you would tell them if you were there in person.

Guest Expectations

Your tone, the way your house is set up, your information sheet, your house rules, your greetings, the phone conversations you have had all will combine to define the extent of your hospitality. They have told the guest what to expect from you.

For your own sake, learn to tread a fine line between open-handedness and the limitations in your house rules—which are made for your protection. In your eagerness to be a good host, do not promise more than you are happy to deliver, simply to help your B&B look better. If you overextend yourself, you will find you can never relax or get behind-the-scenes chores done.

Define your hospitality to fit your life style. Are you going to treat guests as part of the family, and include them in your activities or at your dinner table? Do you want to personally welcome them when they come back in the evening and invite them to have coffee? Or, would you rather they went their own way? If you are by choice doing a low volume business, then you can take more time for each guest and lavish a more personal hospitality if you wish.

Some hosts will let guests use their refrigerator or make coffee in the kitchen, or have various degrees of kitchen privileges. Some guests may have special diet needs and hope to use your refrigerator to keep special foods. A working host may allow guests such latitude and yet never see much of them, but if you are home they could get in your way. What is convenient for you may not be convenient for another host whose daytime schedule is different from yours.

Guests are paying for a bedroom and bath, breakfast and probably the use of your living room or grounds. Beyond that, offer only what is realistic and comfortable for you. Then you and your guests can relax and enjoy yourselves within these limits.

Protecting Your Privacy

When there are two hosts, it is less hassle, and each can take turns being "off-duty." If you are the only one, then it all falls on you. Whether you are hosting solo or in tandem, make sure part of the house is not open to guests. Reserve a place you can go to sit, relax, lie down, or do your own chores and paper work.

Learn to do so, when needed, simply by excusing yourself: you control the situation. And if you are tired, don't make guest reservations; say you are full and place the booking with your backup network.

Keep to the check-in and check-out and breakfast times you have set, so you have time for yourself. You will be more comfortable and a better host if you are not feeling harassed. Staying in your home really could be a memorable part of someone's trip—our guests have told us that on occasion—so be up to your full potential and have the satisfaction afterwards of having done things the way you wanted to.

What to Expect from Guests

As each new guest arrives, you may wonder how much or how little attention to give them. They will make this clear to you. Do not hover around: they may want to be left alone. Do not hurry them, either. In general, take your cue from the guests.

Some guests clear the table themselves and take dishes out to the kitchen and offer to wash them. Some ask you to sit and talk with them while they eat breakfast. Others may talk only to their fellow guests, and be less friendly with you; they simply want to be treated as paying guests.

Learn also to be patient. You are dealing with the public, and people can sometimes be annoying or demanding. Enjoy the great guests and take in your stride the—only infrequent—disappointments.

By the end of a weekend we usually have had interesting conversation, learned some new things, and often made new friends. We have been invited to visit Europe, the United Kingdom and many places in the United States. We have met a great variety of people and shared their lives for a bit, as they have shared ours. It does happen that hosts and guests become fast friends over a weekend. You must be realistic, however, and not expect every weekend to be this way.

Complaints

There are a number of ways you can minimize guest dissatisfaction. Be sure to make it very clear in your brochure or telephone conversation exactly what you are offering—the kind of house, rooms, town, bath, breakfast. If you are specific, you will attract the kind of person who wants your kind of accommodations, and will not be disappointed because they were expecting something else.

At the beginning of each stay always ask guests if everything is okay or there is anything else they need. For example, some people like an extra pillow and do not sleep well unless they are comfortably set-up. Mention that extra pillows are available. Being flexible and specific defuses potential problems.

You cannot, of course, anticipate everything, especially unexpected situations. We had a complaint on a very hot day last summer when a fuse blew and the fans stopped running. The complaint was quite legitimate and the fuse was replaced, with our apologies and thanks to the guests for being such good sports, which they were. Handle whatever comes up with an immediate response, and do not seem indifferent even to trivial things.

Some hosts prefer to have a complaint or rating sheet in each room, which they ask the guest to fill out before leaving. We have given suggestions for a "guest satisfaction" check list in Chapter 5. As we said, if you join a reservation service organization, you may be asked by the RSO to use such sheets as a way of checking on your overall B&B operation.

Sometimes guests write comments in the guest book but these are never uncomplimentary, so they are not really a critique. As they are leaving, guests are likely to tell you spontaneously what they particularly enjoyed. This, of course does not tell you what they disliked, but you cannot be everything to everyone, and if you are running a B&B well and efficiently, and it is clean and functional, then you are unlikely to get many complaints.

Payment

Don't be shy about asking for payment. It will not ruin your relationship with your guest, and they too usually are glad to get the transaction over with. Don't forget to deduct the deposit if they sent one.

Make it clear to them when you want them to pay. Some hosts make payment a part of registration because they find it awkward to ask for money after having become acquainted. Some hosts present a bill at breakfast, or as guests are leaving. If you have not made it clear, guests usually will ask when you want payment. Some guests insist on paying when they register.

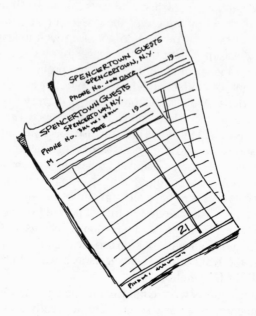

If you belong to an RSO, the guests may have pre-paid the organization before arriving at your house, so you will not be collecting money. Many hosts prefer this arrangement. We present the bill when guests are leaving, and have found that this works out well. The timing seems right: a part of saying goodbye.

You will soon find a time and tone you feel comfortable with when collecting your fee. Thereafter, don't let payment intrude further on your weekend. After the first couple of times hosting guests, you will feel less awkward about taking money. Having done the work of preparing the room and breakfast, answering questions, and generally hosting, your fee will seem well-deserved.

Be sure to make clear to guests how they may pay. Some hosts take only cash, some take cash or checks. Some even have a credit card affiliation. (Before you get involved in such an arrangement, check out how much it will cost you and if you can afford it. Call American Express, or contact VISA or Mastercard through your local bank, to find out what terms they offer small businesses in your area.) If you have a cash-only policy, state this in your brochure and house rules, so guests still will have cash when they are ready to leave. Otherwise, they may spend it on other things and expect to be able to give you a check.

Most B&B hosts confirm that they have never had a check returned. But, if you are more comfortable with cash only, then stick to that, and don't forget to settle the phone bill as well before departure time.

7
Breakfast

How you as a host approach breakfast will depend on how much time you have for your guests. If you are a working host, or doing a very high-volume business, your breakfast procedure and menu will be less leisurely and varied than those of a host with more time to spend.

Breakfast Variations

A continental breakfast—for example, roll or toast or donuts plus juice and coffee—is the B&B fare served most often. Some hosts enhance this by making it an all-you-can-eat continental breakfast: as much coffee as you can drink; large glasses of juice with refills; all the toast, jam and butter you want; and maybe seasonal fruit on the table.

Some hosts offer both a continental and, at an additional fee, a full breakfast, and let guests choose. Many hosts feel that breakfast is a big part of their hospitality. They have breakfast specialties and say so in their advertising. The choice is up to you.

Some B&B writers speculate that the traditional continental breakfast is a possible weakness of B&B, because many travelers really want a full breakfast. We offer both a continental and a full breakfast and only about three percent of our guests have opted for the latter. Almost every guest has chosen the continental. Apparently, getting breakfast as part of the room price, rather than paying extra for a full breakfast has appealed to them.

Serving Your Guests

Hosts vary not only in what they serve but in how they serve it. We have stayed in a B&B where coffee, two small donuts, and paper cups of juice were left anonymously in the hall outside our room. We ate in the room. It was not our favorite B&B breakfast.

In other B&Bs we have been told beforehand the hours breakfast is available and gone at our leisure into the dining room to find coffee on a hot plate, English muffins and butter and jam alongside an electric toaster oven, and pitchers of juice on the sideboard. The hosts checked in now and then to see that all was well, while we guests chatted with each other around the table.

Other B&B hosts serve their guests individually at a time agreed upon. Most serve in the dining room, some in the kitchen, and some will serve breakfast-in-bed to their guests. Many also serve outside on a balcony or patio when weather permits.

Some hosts never eat with guests, others do so if asked, and some always do. We usually leave guests alone to share their own conversation unless they are the only person or couple in residence. Then it is hospitable to pass through the dining room to see if they want our company or conversation while they are eating. Often they do, because this is a time when they are picking up facts about the area: real estate agents; distances to places they are going that day, and so on. We have never seen, in our own or any other B&B, a guest bring a book to read at the breakfast table. Conversation seems looked forward to and expected.

We serve in the dining room, at the time specified on the breakfast check sheet. We stick to the scheduled time even if we do not hear sounds of stirring from the guest room, for we know that the aroma of perking coffee rouses guests very quickly. We deviate from this procedure only when we have very early risers, such as hunters. Then, the night before we set the table, fill the electric percolator, ready to be turned on, put some Danish and donuts under a cover or cake holder and leave juice and cream on the top shelf of the refrigerator in plain view. This avoids us getting up at 4 A.M.

Attractiveness and Variety

We have found that one can offer an attractive continental breakfast without involved baking or cooking, by stressing variety and freshness. Coffee is always freshly brewed, never instant. Butter is fresh (margarine is never served). Cream is real; jam or jelly is homemade. If we don't bake that day, then Danish or croissants are warmed up in a covered frying pan with a brushing of butter in the bottom, so they smell and taste fresh from the oven. Tea is made in individual pots for any guest who prefers it to coffee. We offer a choice of both regular English teas and herbal

and spice teas, and toast and jam with Danish or donuts or muffins. We serve fruit that is in season: peaches; melon; raspberries, if we can pick them ourselves; pears and grapes. In winter we depend upon apples and other available fruit.

Many B&B hosts cook up a storm. They bake and serve delicious dishes for breakfast: homemade breads and muffins, casseroles and glorious egg dishes. If you are a host who enjoys cooking, B&B gives you an opportunity to demonstrate your talents to an appreciative breakfast audience. If you serve special breakfast dishes, mention this in your brochure or guide listing.

Keep in mind that some guests may have allergies or some may be vegetarians. Many of our guests have had citrus allergies, so we keep tomato and V8 juice on hand to provide alternatives to orange juice. Granola and cereals, with fruit added if you wish, and cheese, eggs and sometimes poached fish are breakfast dishes welcome to vegetarians. Always remember to check out guests' food preferences so that they are not disappointed by sitting down to a breakfast they can only eat part of. It's a deflating way for them to begin the day.

Always set an attractive breakfast table. We have chosen not to use paper plates, napkins or cups. We use tablecloths, cloth napkins, china settings, and nice flatware. We put flowers, dried or real, or a plant on the table. Guests always react to a well-set table, even before they are served their food. They enjoy eating this way—many are too busy to take the time at home—and they regularly comment to us on how nice or elegant the table looks. If you do not want to use a tablecloth, then try mats and napkins that match and have an attractive design or color.

Whether you are a working or at home host, have your breakfast setup organized. Know the night before what tablecloths or mats, dishes, and flatware you are using. Double-check them for spotlessness. Know your menu and have things easily at hand. Check things out beforehand wherever you can. Avoid last-minute discoveries: not having enough coffee; or no tea bags; or having spots on the tablecloth; or not having enough mats or napkins the same color.

Remember that what you use to set the table may be influenced by the number of guests you are serving that morning. Unexpected, last-minute arrivals should not disturb or disorganize your breakfast plans. Be ready for anything. And do start preparations well before the time guests have specified for breakfast. Sometimes they surprise you by coming down slightly early because something from the kitchen smelled so good.

However busy you are, do not stint on breakfast. Even if you cannot be there with your guests, make sure the table is set nicely, and they have a generous and appetizing breakfast. It is an important part of Bed and Breakfast and should never be minimized.

Recipes

There are many things to serve for breakfast, and everyone probably has some favorite recipes or menu ideas of their own. Following are recipes collected from some of the cooks, hosts and homemakers here in Columbia County, and also a few from New York City friends. If you are fresh out of ideas, these should help you along.

Top-of-Stove

Rita Stewart's Eggs Bermudiana

6 eggs, well beaten
½ cup grated cheddar cheese
½ cup tomato soup, concentrated (not diluted)
½ cup half and half
Salt and pepper

Mix all ingredients and beat well. Scramble (cook) over medium heat, stirring constantly with wooden spoon until of soft consistency. Serve with breakfast sausage and toast points, as an excellent brunch dish.
Serves 4.

Neal Thompson's Tex-Mex Eggs

3 bellpeppers (all green or 1 red, 2 green)
2 medium-sized bermuda onions
2 large tomatoes
2 tablespoons margarine
4-6 eggs

Melt margarine in a skillet that can be covered with secure lid (for steaming). Slice peppers, onions and tomatoes thinly (⅛″) and sauté in margarine until tomatoes are soft and cooked into purée. (Peppers and onions will be a little firmer but softening.) Break eggs on surface of mixture and cover with lid (preferably glass so you can watch eggs without having to lift lid). When egg yolks have turned white and egg whites appear firm, remove from heat and serve immediately. Individual eggs can be served on English muffins, toast or by themselves. Salt and pepper to taste. Mushrooms may also be added for substance, especially if for an evening meal. Add or subtract amount of peppers, onions and tomatoes as needed for amount of eggs. (Note: Do not use iron skillet. It will cause eggs to appear black around edges due to interaction of acid in tomatoes with iron.)

Emily McCully's Eggs with Tomato and Leftover Potato

1 scallion
2 tomatoes, cut up
A few cooked potatoes
2 eggs, beaten
¼ cup milk
Fresh herbs as desired

Sauté a scallion in butter. Add tomatoes, and cook until soft. Add slices of cooked potato. Beat the eggs with milk. Add salt and pepper and fresh herbs. To avoid using two pans, cook in a well in the center of the same pan. Serve with homemade bread, toasted.

Emily McCully's Country Eggs Benedict (or Eggs Beatrice)

This dish calls for homemade mayonnaise, which Emily says takes only a couple of minutes to make in a blender.

1 egg
1 teaspoon dry mustard
1 teaspoon salt
1 tablespoon good vinegar
¾ cup oil
Lemon juice

Poached Eggs
Ham Slices, about ¼" or less
English Muffins

To make mayonnaise (this is a mock Hollandaise Sauce), first break one egg into blender. Add mustard and salt. Blend briefly. Add vinegar and blend. Pour oil slowly into blender jar until all is incorporated. Add lemon juice to taste.

Poach as many eggs as needed. Toast English muffins. Put slices of ham on muffins. Add poached egg, and then some of the mayonnaise.

Martha Gilmor's French Toast

Whole grain bread slices cut thick
2 eggs
⅔ cup milk
Salt and pepper
Powdered sugar

Martha thought the ideal French toast is made with good whole grain breads. The crusts should be cut off and the bread really soaked in the egg and milk mixture. Brown both sides of the bread in a well-buttered frying pan (or griddle). Sprinkle with powdered sugar if desired.

Ed Berry's S.O.S.

Some call this recipe "creamed chipped beef," others, "chipped beef gravy." It took the fighting boys of WWII to definitively title it "S.O.S." Ed's wife Ellen has dolled it up so that Ed notes it bears no relationship, hardly, to that served by the mess sargeant.

4 oz. chipped beef, shredded
1½ tablespoons butter
3 scallions or, the white part of one leek or, 4 thin slices of onion.
2 tablespoons green pepper or celery, chopped fine
2 tablespoons flour
1½ cups milk
Pepper
Parsley
Dry sherry (optional)
½ teaspoon dry mustard or, chopped pickles, or capers
2 hard boiled eggs, sliced

Melt butter. Sauté pepper or celery and scallions or onions until translucent. Sprinkle with the flour and cook briefly. Add milk and cook until partially thickened. Add beef and seasonings. Serve on cornbread or toast, garnished with egg slices.
Serves 2.

Penny MacDonald's "Bread Waffles"

This is an ingenious dish which Penny came across in her "American Travels."

Slices of day-old bread
Pancake batter
Maple syrup

Prepare pancake batter according to your own recipe or a mix. Dip bread slices into pancake batter. Fry and serve like waffles, with maple syrup over them.

Terry Roberson's Garlic Fries

4 potatoes, medium sized, unpeeled, thinly sliced
1 onion, medium sized, chopped
3 tablespoons bacon drippings
1 clove garlic, minced
Salt and pepper to taste

In a large skillet add bacon drippings and garlic. Cook over medium heat for 3-4 minutes. Add potatoes, onions, salt and pepper. Cover and cook over medium heat for 15 minutes loosening potatoes 2 or 3 times. Uncover. Turn potatoes. Cook 10-15 minutes over medium-high heat, loosening potatoes 2 or 3 times. Potatoes should be tender and brown.
Serves 4.

Isabel Zander's Michigan Scrapple

Isabel's recipe card says she used to make this with 10 cents worth of pork shoulder. In today's terms this translates into:

¾-1 cup pork, lean, shredded, cooked
White cornmeal
Water
Salt and pepper; other seasonings as desired
1 egg, beaten
2-3 tablespoons butter

Make scrapple by first making cornmeal. Boil meal and water (as per directions on cornmeal box) in the quantity you desire. When it is slightly cool, put in the pork and seasonings. (Season firmly, as this is a bland, midwestern scrapple.) Put in an ice cube tray (without the divisions) to cool in the refrigerator, not the freezer. Cover the top so it doesn't dry out. When ready to prepare, cut into about ¼ inch slices. Don't make them too thick or they will be mushy, not crispy. Dip in the egg, cover both sides, and fry in a buttered pan until crisp and brown on both sides.

Jean Laurain's Omelette Forestere

8 eggs
½ pound smoked ham, diced
½ pound mushrooms, diced (not too thick)
3 oz. (⅓ cup) milk
3 tablespoons butter
½ cup chopped parsley
3 scallions, if desired, including green parts, cut into ¼-½″ pieces
Salt and pepper to taste

Keep eggs out overnight so they are at room temperature. Use two stoneware pans, one larger. In one pan, with some of the butter, saute the ham, mushrooms and scallions. Don't let them get too brown. In a bowl, beat eggs with milk, parsley, salt and pepper. In the other pan, with the rest of the butter melted to warm it, add ½ the egg mixture. Put in the warm mushrooms/ham/scallion mixture, and then the rest of the egg mixture. Don't cook over too hot a flame. Use a medium temperature, briefly. Use a spatula to separate around the edge. When the bottom is hard, fold in half or turn ¼ and ¼, etc. to fold. Then you can turn the omelette over so the seam can't be seen. Don't overcook, it should be juicy.

Jean and his wife Bea serve this with juice, marmalade and toast. And, if it is a festive breakfast or brunch, a French sparkling wine such as Vin Mousseau.

Casseroles

Peggy Haskel's "Sleeze"

Peggy says this is medium-hot to taste, with this amount of peppers.

4 English muffins, split and buttered
1 lb. bulk sausage
8 eggs, beaten
½ cup sour cream
½ lb. sharp cheddar cheese, grated
1 3 oz. can lemon peppers (to taste) (or, chilie peppers if desired)

Butter muffins and place buttered side down in buttered casserole. Cook sausage; crumble and drain. Sprinkle sausage over muffins. Beat eggs, add sour cream. Pour over sausage and muffins. Grate cheese and add peppers. Sprinkle over top. Cover and leave in refrigerator overnight (or 6-8 hours). Bake in 350 degree oven for 35-40 minutes. Cut in squares to serve.
Serves 8-10.

Marge Schoonover's Ham and Cheese Souffle

8 slices white bread, cubed
1½ cups ham, chopped
1½ cups cheddar cheese, grated
1 small onion, minced
Salt and pepper to taste

10 eggs
2½ cups milk
½ stick butter or margarine, melted
2 teaspoons dry mustard
½ cup parmesan cheese, grated
Paprika

In buttered 2 quart souffle dish, layer ⅓ bread, ½ ham, cheddar cheese, onion, salt, pepper. Repeat layers, top with last ⅓ bread. Beat eggs, add milk, cooled melted butter, dry mustard. Mix well. Pour over bread in dish. Sprinkle with parmesan and paprika. Refrigerate overnight (covered). Bake uncovered 350 degrees for one hour. Serve immediately.
Serves 4-6.

Rita Stewart's Spinach Frittata

3 tablespoons pure olive oil
1 cup scallions or shallots, thinly sliced
10 eggs
1 cup raw spinach, finely chopped (½ pound)
⅓ cups grated parmesan cheese
2 tablespoons parsley, chopped
1 clove garlic, crushed
1 level teaspoon salt
¼ teaspoon pepper

Preheat oven to 350 degrees. Heat oil in 10 inch heavy skillet with heat resistant handle. Add scallions and sauté until tender (5 minutes). In large bowl combine remaining ingredients with wire whisk or fork. Beat until well blended. Turn into skillet with onion. Cook over low heat. Lift from bottom with a spatula as the eggs set, about 3 minutes. Bake uncovered 10 minutes or until top is set. With spatula loosen from bottom and around edge. Slide onto serving platter. Cut into wedges. (Chopped green pepper or chopped tomatoes may be added to scallions for variety.)
Serves 4-6.

Thelma Hall's Cheese Strata

12 slices Pepperidge Farm thin bread, crusts removed
½ pound sharp cheddar cheese, grated
4 eggs
2½ cups milk
½ teaspoon mustard
1 teaspoon seasoned salt
1 tablespoon dry minced onion
½ teaspoon salt
Dash of cayenne
Dash of pepper

Place 6 bread slices in the bottom of a 12"x8" or 13"x9" greased pan. Cover with cheese and onion. Top with remaining bread slices. Beat eggs with mustard and seasonings, pour over all. Cover and let stand overnight in refrigerator (up to 24 hours). (Baste several times while in refrigerator. Keep tightly covered with plastic wrap until time for oven.) Cook for 1 hour, or until evenly browned, at 325 degrees.
Serves 4-6.

Quick Breads

Frieda Gabel's Rhubarb Bread

¾ cup brown sugar
1 egg
⅓ cup vegetable oil
½ cup milk
½ teaspoon each salt, baking soda, vanilla
1¼ cup flour
1 cup diced rhubarb

Beat sugar, egg, and oil. Add in salt, soda, vanilla and milk. Mix in flour, then stir in rhubarb. Use greased pan. Bake at 350 degrees for 60 minutes.

Frieda Gabel's Crunchy Oat and Cranberry Muffins

¾ cup all-purpose flour
¾ cup whole wheat flour
1 cup old-fashioned oatmeal
½ cup brown sugar
1 tablespoon baking powder
1 teaspoon cinnamon
1 cup fresh or frozen cranberries
½ stick butter or oleo
1 egg
1 cup milk

Heat oven to 425 degrees and butter muffin cups or paper cups. In a bowl blend dry ingredients well. Melt butter and, off heat, stir in the milk and beat in the egg. Stir liquid mixture into dry ingredients and when well-mixed stir in cranberries. Fill muffin cups, bake 15-20 minutes and let stand 5 minutes before removing from tin. Dip tops in granulated sugar. These freeze well and can be made ahead of time and then defrosted when needed. Reheats well. Makes one dozen.

Hazel Ball's Twin Mountain Muffins

This is a very old muffin recipe. Hazel's favorite.

¼ cup butter
¼ cup sugar
½ teaspoon salt
1 egg
1 cup milk
2 cups flour
5 teaspoons baking powder

Cream butter and sugar together. Add well-beaten egg. Measure flour after one sifting, and then sift again with baking powder. Add latter to first mixture, alternating with milk. Bake in greased muffin pans for 25 minutes at 400 degrees.

Carol Reamer's Blueberry Buckle

Carol and Tom run the Spencertown Country Store which carries a variety of home-baked goodies. And if you were going to Carol's for breakfast, this is what she'd probably serve.

CAKE
½ cup butter or margarine
½ cup sugar
1 egg, beaten
2 cups white flour
2½ teaspoons baking powder
¼ teaspoon salt
½ cup milk
2 teaspoons lemon juice
2 cups blueberries
   (fresh or frozen)

TOPPING
¼ cup butter or magarine
½ teaspoon cinnamon
½ cup white flour
½ cup sugar

Cream butter and sugar; add egg; beat until light. Sift together the dry ingredients; add to the creamed mixture alternately with milk. Spread the batter in a greased 9"x9" pan. Toss the berries with the lemon juice; sprinkle them over the batter. Make the topping by mixing ingredients together with a pastry blender or fork; pour over the berries. Bake in preheated oven at 350° for 1 hour or until done. This is especially good if served warm.

Kent Brown's Cranberry-Apple Pudding

This is Kent's most requested breakfast dish over at his Thornberry Inn in Canaan, N.Y.

1 cup flour
¼ teaspoon salt
1 teaspoon baking soda
½ teaspoon cinnamon
½ teaspoon freshly grated nutmeg
Dash of allspice and cloves
¼ cup (half of a stick) unsalted butter, softened
1 cup sugar
1 large egg
1 cup grated apple (cored and peeled)
1 cup fresh whole cranberries
1 teaspoon grated orange rind
½ cup chopped walnuts

Preheat oven to 325 degrees. Butter and flour a 9″ or 10″ tube mold pan or bundt pan.

In a small bowl, combine flour, soda, salt and spices. In a larger bowl, cream together the butter and sugar; beat in the egg with a wire whisk. Stir in the apple, cranberries and orange rind; blend in dry ingredients, then stir in nuts. Pour into prepared pan and bake at 325 degrees for one hour (sometimes an hour and fifteen minutes in the smaller pan). Cool slightly before slicing. This pudding freezes well. (Defrost thoroughly at room temperature before reheating.)

Other fruit can be substituted for the cranberries, though with less tangy result. For example, blueberries, raspberries, strawberries or a combination of strawberries and finely chopped rhubarb. Carrots can be substituted for all or part of the apple.

Granola and Fruit

Mitzi Lobdell's Granola

6 cups regular oats
½ cup brown sugar
¾ cup wheat germ
½ cup flaked coconut (optional)
¼ cup sesame seeds
1 cup bran
1 cup chopped walnuts
½ cup nonfat dry milk
⅔ cup vegetable oil
⅔ cup honey
2 tablespoons water
1½ teaspoons vanilla
1 cup raisins

In a large bowl combine oats, brown sugar, wheat germ, bran, coconut, seeds, nuts and dry milk. In another bowl combine honey, oil, water and vanilla. (Heat honey if hard.) Add to oat mixture and stir to coat all ingredients. Turn mixture into two large shallow pans. Heat in 300 degree oven for 25-35 minutes until lightly toasted. Stir twice during heating. Stir while cooling. Add raisins. Store in tightly sealed container. Makes about 14 cups.

Mrs. Doane's Pinecot, A Fruit Syrup

1 pound apricots
1 pound canned pineapple, or fresh pineapple
3 cups sugar

Make a syrup with the pineapple juice and sugar. Cut or grind apricots and pineapple and cook together with the juice and sugar for a few minutes. Be careful, as it burns easily.

Lorna Moore's Dried Fruit Preserve

This is nice in winter when fresh fruits are not as available for cooking.

1 pound of dried apricots, prunes, apples, pears, and raisins
   (No dates or figs.)
Water
Lemon or orange

Place dried fruit in a good-sized pan and cover with water. Slice a clean lemon or orange into thin rounds and add them. Bring to a boil, then simmer about an hour. Serve as a preserve on muffins or pancakes, or wrapped in plain yogurt.

Lorraine Zagarola's Fruit Cup

A good fresh fruit cup can be made using the juice of grapefruit and oranges as a citrus base. Cut the segments out of one large, juicy grapefruit and 2 oranges, remove all pits and membrane and then squeeze into the same bowl any juice left in the peel. Add whole blueberries and white, seedless grapes; quarter segments of strawberries and bing cherries; and small pieces of cantaloupe, watermelon, nectarine and peach. All these add color. Squeeze any juice out of peels or skins to add to liquid base. Banana slices can be added as a garnish just before serving. Texture is enhanced with crisp pieces of apple and pear. Be sure to add enough other fruit to the citrus so that the fruit cup is balanced between having enough liquid but not being too acidic.

Lorna Moore's Fresh Fruit; and Fruit with Yogurt

While fruit looks pretty served whole, it is more attractive cut up and laid out decoratively on a plate. Oranges peeled and segmented; peeled thin wedges of melon or pears; crisp apple wedges with their green skins still on; small grape clusters; sliced bananas; halved pomagranates; small, whole apricots or peaches. Some combination of pieces of these fruits, nicely arranged, is very appealing.

Putting pieces of fresh fruit into plain (unsweetened) yogurt and coating every piece by gently stirring the mixture makes a delicious dish for breakfast or any other meal. In winter, when fresh fruits are not as available, a similar dish can be created with frozen fruits (sweetened strawberries or raspberries). If left in the yogurt overnight in a covered bowl in the refrigerator, the berries will defrost and the mixture can be served for breakfast.

PART IV
Marketing

8

Publicizing on Your Own

There are many ways to spread the word about your B&B. Those that are free or very inexpensive are emphasized in this chapter. Before trying out any one of these methods, balance its cost against its income potential. Establish that you really need it. Is it suited to your particular circumstances and area, or would something else be better fitted? Weigh cost, suitability and the effort involved before you act. Also, before beginning your marketing and publicity efforts, consider what volume you want for your B&B. Do not publicize so heavily that you cannot handle the resultant volume.

Many of these advertising methods require a "promotional piece" that you can pin to bulletin boards, hand to people, mail, and so forth. Whether it is a business card, a flyer, or a brochure depends, again, on what is appropriate for your particular circumstances.

Ways to Make Your B&B Known

Making your B&B known is a building process which can involve some or all of these elements:

- Defining clientele.
- Developing credibility and creating an image.
- Local informal contacts, local referrals, word-of-mouth.
- Formal contacts, both local and over a broader area.
- Exchanges with similar businesses.
- Guidebook listings.
- Listing in the local telephone book.
- Joining a reservation service organization (RSO).
- Paid ads.
- Repeat-business and word-of-mouth on a broader level.

You must do the first two steps. The last will follow as part of the on-going process. Your use of the others will depend upon your individual situation: whether you are in the city or the country; whether you join other organizations or an RSO, and the volume of business for which you are aiming. To what degree you use each procedure, and how you combine them, is a matter of common sense and appropriateness. Remember that most of these are on-going processes. You must keep them up; they are not usually one-shot efforts.

We will discuss RSO and guidebook listings in the next chapter. In this chapter we focus on those things you can do yourself, locally, to help publicize your B&B.

Defining Your Preferred Clientele

Marketing your own home is more personal than marketing something like soap powder, but the principle is much the same. You must define and locate your market and then sell to it. Where you are located, what kind of home you have, and the kind of host you are will help refine the definition of your target market.

Obviously, you want to attract people who are interested in staying overnight in your area, but within that group you can make a number of more specific definitions. For example, you do, or do not, want smokers, pets, children under 12, drinkers, hunters, skiers, etc. In your promotional pieces, state your preferences clearly. Present your image in such a way as to limit inquiries from people you'd rather not have. But keep in mind that each limitation also may limit your volume of business.

Next, think about your home and to whom it might appeal as well as to whom you'd like it to appeal. Is it very posh, handsome, stately, elegant? Is it modest, plain, comfortable, homey, functional? Is it full of kids, family-oriented, folksy? Is it charming, cozy, old-fashioned, does it have some antiques?

And what about you? Are you looking for new friends to talk and share with? Do you want to have breakfast and dinner with your guest, or a drink in the evening before dinner? Or, do you expect them to be very self-sufficient? All of these things will determine the tone of any publicity you write, and your description of yourself and your home will be influential in determining who responds.

If you are open to a broad clientele, you can list in a guidebook, with travel agents, in the telephone directory, on bulletin boards, and so on. If you want to screen for a very specific, limited clientele, you may opt for locating guests only through an RSO (reservation service organization) which will match guests to your specifications. So decide early on how broad your hosting will be as it will influence your selection of publicity methods. Once you have a picture in mind of your ideal clientele, you can start selling your B&B.

Developing Credibility

The next step is to develop credibility with all those who can help publicize your B&B. This means creating belief in yourself, in your B&B, and, if you run an RSO, your organization. A high-volume B&B will not be functioning in a vacuum. Especially in smaller towns, many people around you may be aware of it in one way or another. If you have strong credibility within the community, it will help you to get customers.

People will refer guests to you if they think it will reflect well on them. Local businesses (e.g., merchants, museums, performing arts centers, restaurant owners, real estate brokers) like visitors to stay in the area and remain reasonably happy while doing so. If they think you are well-prepared and offer a pleasant experience to their own customers, they will recommend your B&B. If they have doubts about you, they may refer customers to someone else. If there are several good alternatives, it's a toss-up; but if you are not credible, then you've lost your competitive edge.

Show everyone that you are serious. Be specific in discussing your B&B. Have an exact date for your opening and be ready by that date. Know what your rates are going to be and advise those people who might be interested. Sound positive and committed. Make it very apparent that this is a serious business to you.

Explain B&B to people if they do not understand it. Invite them to see the room(s) you are renting. Set your image. Perhaps you can get the local newspaper to announce your opening. Join the chamber of commerce. In all your public dealings appear organized and determined. It will make those around you believe in your enterprise.

Using Local Contacts

There are many local contacts that can be invaluable for no-cost advertising. Ask to leave your card, flyer or brochure in local places of business—at the receptionist's desk or the cashier's counter—and in return place theirs on a table by your front door or in your guest rooms. Many local stores will have bulletin boards on which you can pin a card or flyer.

Display menus from local restaurants. If you call a restaurant to make a reservation for your guests, let the restaurant owner know you have sent him business.

Consider who is likely to have visitors or guests from out-of-town, such as hospitals, schools, colleges and nursing homes. Train and bus stations, libraries and laundromats are places with a constant flow of people. Even local hotels or motels might refer guests to your B&B when they are completely filled. Ask to display your publicity material in any of these places.

Keep talking about your B&B. For example, tell local beauty parlor owners and they will tell their customers. Ask people to spread the word. This is a sure way to get broad local dissemination. And allow time for word to get around. By the end of our first year, we saw that half our bookings came via word-of-mouth from local contacts. As our guidebook listing began to attract guests the second year, word-of-mouth referrals adjusted to about 40% of bookings. It is a very solid method of attracting guests at little or no cost.

Using Broader Contacts

Another source of inexpensive and effective publicity may be a newspaper or magazine story. Many newspapers are interested in the burgeoning B&B movement. One of your papers might write an article about your business. Our local paper did a long picture story about us to acquaint people county-wide with B&B.

Some papers have a business section and will do an article on new businesses in the area. Some have a summer calendar and tourism section which comes out weekly and lists places for people to stay in the area. All these are free to you and will establish your credibility as well as give wider publicity.

The local chamber of commerce—either in your city, or, if you are in a rural area, the one located in the county seat—can also be helpful. Besides displaying your promotional piece in their tourism rack, some might mail it out when they respond to specific inquiries from persons intending to visit or stay in the area.

In some areas the chamber of commerce does an annual or seasonal volume-mailing. They usually will include group but not individual pieces in this mailing. You might consider joining other B&Bs in having a flyer printed in very large quantities to be included. The chamber may expect you to share the mailing cost to some small extent—perhaps 1% of the total. Remember that by having brochures or cards printed up and mailed in this quantity you increase expenses, so do have some sense of the minimum return you can expect before you do this. However, if there are other B&Bs in the area and you all pay for a joint flyer and mailing, it will be less expensive. But it is not recommended as an initial advertising step. Wait until you have tried your wings a bit before making such an outlay.

List with your state department of tourism, which gets a fair number of tourist enquiries. Rather than giving them an address, you may wish to give only a telephone number, since giving an address could eliminate some screening. The same procedure could be followed with the chamber of commerce. Also, you might wish to make an arrangement with a travel bureau, many of whom are now working with B&Bs. Of course they will charge a commission, but you will not pay anything until they send you a guest. The arrangement you make with a travel bureau should be clearly defined and understood.

Search out B&Bs in adjacent cities, counties or states. Write asking them to exchange flyers. You can display each other's flyer in your B&B in order to pick up people traveling in the broader geographic area.

Listing in the Yellow Pages

As of this writing, the Yellow Pages are including in their new "B&B" section only the names of those groups whose individual members offer B&B accommodations. If you operate a group or an umbrella organization for a group of B&Bers, you can be included in the Yellow Pages under this heading. If you are an individual B&B, you will be placed under "Hotels and Motels" in the Yellow Pages. Since few people at present are likely to look for "B&B" in the Yellow Pages, you will be more visible in the motel section for now, anyway.

Usually you are entitled to one free listing in the Yellow Pages if you have a business telephone. This listing frequently produces last-minute calls from people who cannot find a motel room, and does eliminate some screening. We have gotten some nice guests through the Yellow Pages, but they have accounted for only about 7% of our total bookings. The percentage might be higher in a very heavy tourist area.

Paying for Advertising

Since ads are expensive, you should be very selective in placing them, and very careful of how you phrase them. If there is some particular draw to your place or your area, relate it both to your ad copy and to where you place the ad. For instance, if there is good bird-watching you might place the ad in a magazine like *Audubon,* which attracts birders. A mild climate, or the ability to get around your area without a car might be appealing to retirees.

Go to your public library and consult *Ayers, Ulrich's,* or *Standard Rate and Data Service* to see what magazines or papers are subscribed to by the kinds of people you think your place might appeal to: history buffs, tennis players, skiers, families, artists, kids, music fans, hunters. Place the ad only in those magazines or papers your target population seems most likely to read.

In some cases your B&B might better be advertised in a general way, such as under the headings: "Country Inns and Lodgings" or "Bed and Breakfast Accommodations" in the classified ad section of the newspaper. Small, classified ads are, of course, always cheaper than the larger space ads.

Unless you are part of a larger cooperating group or have a great many rooms, be very cautious about buying ad space. Some of the other methods listed here are better uses of your ad money.

Repeat Business

Repeat business is a direct result of the traveler's experience with you the first time around. It is pleasant to get repeat business, since the unknowns are removed for both host and guest—presumably the earlier visit was good or they would not have returned. We found that by our third year we were averaging about 25% in repeat bookings.

Broader word-of-mouth also comes over time. It is a kind of geometric progression of your original and continuing publicity efforts. More people, including those who stay there, mention your place to more people, and so on and so on. The message goes beyond the local area and may also involve a brochure or business card being passed on, because people want an address and phone number to refer to.

Repeat business and word-of-mouth referrals result from "free" advertising—the overall effects of operating your B&B in a satisfactory way.

Evaluating Publicity

Always ask your guests where they heard about you. This will give you an idea of the effectiveness of your various publicity methods. Then, if need be, you can modify where you put your time and money. You can better judge if guidebook listing fees, membership fees and commission policies are just paying for themselves or bringing a respectable return. Perhaps you can eliminate some.

Our experience suggests that, at least initially, advertising money should be spent on one or two inexpensive guidebook listings, and on a promotional piece. A major effort should go into making your B&B known locally through the no-cost or low-cost efforts we have discussed. Your printed material can be posted, mailed, given out, left on counters or whatever. Persisting in these efforts and expanding your contacts will be very important.

Writing Your Own Publicity

If you feel uncomfortable writing publicity, just take it very slowly. A business card is simple. A flyer, brochure or descriptive ad usually is a little more work. Check out one of the guidebooks we mention in the Resource section. There you will see many examples of how hosts describe their B&Bs.

Study the copy of our brochure on the next pages. It contains specific kinds of information you can write up. Analyze the way we have set them up and adapt them to your circumstances.

Cut the writing down to size. Write a few sentences about your own B&B for each topic we cover in the brochure. Spend a couple of hours smoothing and refining these, and soon you will have plenty of good text for an ad or brochure of your own. Ask a friend to look at it and help you—especially to be objective. Don't exaggerate and then regret it for as long as the publicity is in print. Don't be too modest, either.

Writing publicity for your B&B will help finalize your policy, by formalizing in writing: whether you take children, smokers, or drinkers; your deposit, refund, and seasonal discount policy, and so on.

Your promotional pieces will shape your image. The design and printface of a business card will convey some kind of picture to a potential guest. A line-drawing or logo or the choice of type-face in your brochure will do the same. Think carefully about how these things should look before making final arrangements with the printer.

Printed words, whether on business cards, brochures, flyers, or ads, help build your credibility. They make a positive impression on people, give something concrete to refer to, and they have many uses over an extended period. We particularly recommend preparing a brochure if you are aiming for high volume. A brochure is invaluable to the self-publicizing host or even those who join RSOs.

Producing a Single-sheet Brochure

In our brochure we have divided the text into three areas. First, there is a description of the house, both its physical appearance and its general ambience—its age, furnishings, and what the guest can expect in the way of hospitality within these surroundings. The fact that drinking is allowed, that there are stairs to climb, that the bath is shared, the breakfast details—all are clearly woven into the text along with other descriptive items.

Second, a picture is suggested of how the guest may spend time. Local events, seasonal changes, available activities are described. Third, specific places to visit for various kinds of entertainment—museums, skiing, birdwatching, concerts, historic sites are noted. All three of these "texts" combine to give the guest a good idea of what a stay could be like.

The brochure text also anticipates questions by giving specific information: where can guests get lunch; do they need a car to get to restaurants, and so on. A small map, which we drew and the printer embellished, shows the guest exactly how to find his way to our house. Such a localized map prevents guests dragging around unfamiliar roads trying to find your B&B.

Names, addresses, telephone numbers, time of year open for business are specified. Some hosts add a guest reservation form on one side so the guest can give their name, address and dates preferred and mail it back. Some also provide for checking preferences for single or double beds, number in party, and so on. Your goal for this brochure is to make your B&B sound relaxing, businesslike, attractive, reasonably priced, well-located—all in as few words as possible. If there is local history, or a story to the house, use some of that. Describe to the guest how time might be spent (walking in the woods, browsing through enchanting local

SPENCERTOWN GUESTS

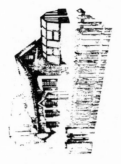

SPENCERTOWN

COLUMBIA COUNTY

NEW YORK

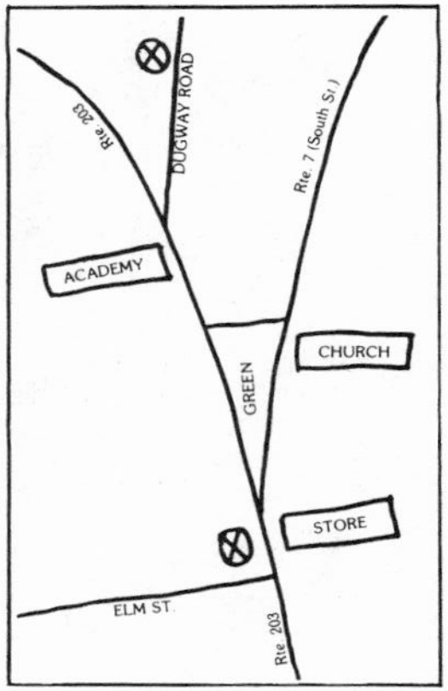

SPENCERTOWN
GUESTS

**OPEN
APRIL TO NOVEMBER**

*Limited Reservations
Rest of Year*

M. & I. ZANDER
Box 122
Spencertown, N.Y. 12165

Map labels: Rte 203 · BUGWAY ROAD · Rte 7 (South St.) · CHURCH · GREEN · Rte 203 · ACADEMY · ELM ST. · STORE

NEARBY PLACES OF INTEREST

Columbia County is graced with many private houses and public museums which are both beautiful and of architectural and historic interest. Highlights among these are the Shaker Museum and Village; Olana, Lindenwald and Steepletop (homes, respectively, of artist Frederick Church, President Martin Van Buren, and poet Edna St. Vincent Millay); the Van Alen House, a seventeenth century Dutch dwelling; and the House of History, now home to the county Historical Society.

The Alan DeVoe Bird Sanctuary offers fine birding and nature walks. Mac-Haydn Theatre and the Spencertown Academy have programs of Broadway, classical and folk music. At Catamount there is downhill skiing, throughout the county there are cross-country trails, and, farther afield, are Butternut, Bosquet, Jiminey Peak, Brodie, Hunter and other large ski areas. Tanglewood and the Boston Symphony are close by, as well as Jacob's Pillow Dance festival and the Berkshire summer theatres.

A day trip to Hyde Park affords a chance to visit the Franklin D. Roosevelt home and Vanderbilt mansion, both with stunning views of the Hudson River. Other day trips might include West Point Military Academy, the Saratoga Race Track, or even New York City via nearby Amtrak. Ask your host for suggestions.

THE GUEST HOUSES

Our Elm Street cottage, an eighteenth century saltbox with attached greenhouse and surrounded by a white picket fence, is located in the center of Spencertown. The living room, with stone fireplace, and the two upstairs guest rooms, are low-ceilinged, with wide-plank floors.

Our 1930's-vintage Golden Hill cottage is located on two acres at the edge of the village, offering fine walks and views along a country road. The panelled living room has a Franklin stove fireplace.

Both houses are pleasantly furnished with antiques, and the guestrooms have comfortable beds, desks and chairs, and good reading lamps. Bath/shower are shared with host. Guests are welcome to relax before the living room fireplaces or to lounge in the yards in warmer weather. Glasses and ice are available for pre-dinner drinks.

A continental breakfast of roll, juice and coffee is included. A full breakfast of bacon, eggs, fresh fruit, cheese and your choice of coffee or various teas is available for an additional fee. The general store supplies good sandwiches, salads and home-baked cookies for lunches, and there are many restaurants within a short car drive.

See enclosed tariff schedules for current rates.

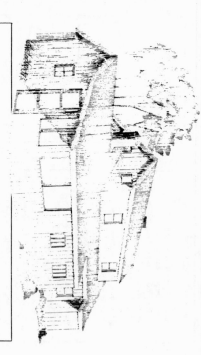

COUNTRY LIVING

Spencertown is a charming village with many old houses, historic Spencertown Academy with its music and art programs, a general store, and a post office. Recently noted by a major news magazine as one of the ten best small towns in America, it offers relaxed days in attractive surroundings. Throughout the county there are pancake breakfasts, barbeques and suppers sponsored by local churches and firehouses; bazaars and bake and tag sales; band concerts and Memorial, July Fourth and Labor Day parades; and a county fair.

There are several major antiques shows annually, as well as arts festivals and exhibitions, horse and carriage shows, and swimming, boating, fishing, hiking, birdwatching, golf, tennis, hunting, cross-country and downhill skiing, antiquing, and theatre-going are available activities. The rolling hills of Columbia County, especially beautiful during the spring apple-blossom time and fall foliage season, provide a scenic accompaniment to sightseeing.

shops, visiting exciting city sites, taking tea in the library, having a drink before the fire, and taking a dip in the pool). Get the flavor of your B&B into the words to convey why it is a good place to stay.

Some hosts include themselves in their publicity. If there is something particularly interesting about you, do not overplay it, but do make reference to it in a way that implies you are a distinctive or unusual host. Choices are enhancing, also. Whether it is four kinds of tea for breakfast, or three different day trips to interesting places, let potential guests know there are pleasant alternatives to choose from.

SPENCERTOWN
GUESTS

Box 122
Spencertown, New York
12165

Telephone
518/392-2358 or 3583

TARIFF SCHEDULE
1983

Daily Rates
Memorial Day through October 15th

One person $18.00

Two persons $25.00

Extra Person $5.00

Plus Tax

Check-out time - 11 a.m.
Check-in time - 1 p.m. to 9 p.m.

A deposit equal to one day's stay is required with your reservation. This is refundable only if notice of cancellation is received one week prior to arrival date.

Balance due upon arrival.
All room rates are subject to change.

Note that we have put rate information, refund and deposit policies, check-in and check-out times on this small, separate card which can be enclosed in the brochure. If you print brochures in fairly large and therefore cheaper quantities, you may not use them all before you want to make a rate change. This way, you have only to reprint the rate card, not the whole brochure.

Working with a Printer

When choosing printers, shop around first. Go to several and ask to see samples of their work that are comparable to what you need. Decide what you like or do not like and try to analyze why. Is it the paper color? The texture of the paper? The kind of lettering used? The spacing? Use the printer's samples to help you specify exactly what you want, then ask for prices using that kind and color of paper, ink and typeface. Get prices for runs of 100 or 500 or 1000. More are cheaper, but don't go for a lot unless you know you can use them over the first few years.

Ask your printer to help you with design layout. Do not use only long blocks of type. Break paragraphs with headings or with illustrations or graphics. Use different-sized type. This will balance the various elements for an overall attractive look.

A nice touch for the brochure is to have a line drawing of your home, inside or out, or both. Some hosts use photographs that do not do justice to the home because they do not reproduce very well. Ask your printer about the possible reproduction quality of an illustration before you use it.

Most printers can do a three-or four-fold printing on both sides of the page for a reasonable cost. Our brochure is a single-sheet, both-sides-printed, three-fold brochure. Whether three- or four-fold, brochures can be designed as self-mailers. The advantages of any one-sheet brochure are first, that it is lightweight for mailing. Second, it is short, not requiring as much writing on your part. Third, it does not cost as much to print as would a larger brochure.

Try to use a local printer if you can. You will have more control over the finished product and the time it takes to do the job. Do not rush in at the last minute to have your brochure or business card printed. You may not get it back in time, or you may wind up with something you do not like the looks of because you didn't think it through. Plan it out before committing it to paper. Ask to see a proof before authorizing the final printing.

Business Cards and Other Printed Materials

If you feel you cannot afford a brochure, then have a business card printed up. It looks professional and helps establish your image and credibility. You can post it or give it out. If you want something to mail to prospective guests, type up pertinent information about your B&B, rubber stamp it with your address and staple or enclose your business card to make it look more professional. Use this system until you feel a brochure is needed and is worth the printing cost.

Some hosts eventually make up postcards of their homes—either line drawings or color photos—and have them imprinted to use for promotion. And, we have been in very successful B&Bs that had their own imprinted stationery and placemats. These things can be quite attractive, but are expensive. Wait until you are doing very well before you spend the money such items cost.

9

Listing with Reservation Service Organizations and in Guidebooks.

Because of zoning restrictions common to residential areas in the United States, B&B proprietors here are not as free to hang out signs and advertise as are those in other countries. Guidebooks and reservation service organizations therefore are immensely important as a means of bringing the names and locations of individual B&Bs to the attention of the traveling public.

Reservation service organizations, booking agencies, referral services—whatever they are called or however they are structured—all have in common the fact that they bring host and guest together for a fee. Guidebooks serve the same purpose.

Early RSOs—some started as house-swapping expediters for vacationers—helped to seek out B&Bs, knitted them into networks, and found guests. Hosts began to advertise as well through the various guidebooks that came into being in the last decade. Many new RSOs also have begun during this period and RSOs, of course, continue to seek out established hosts or develop new ones. Now, in the mid-1980s, hosts have many of both options—guidebooks and RSOs—to use for listing themselves.

Selecting RSOs

RSOs have helped create a greater awareness of B&B in the United States, and have contributed to the expansion of the B&B movement. Whether they use RSOs or not, B&B hosts have several reasons for being indebted to them. Because RSOs have an overview of America's B&B system that most individual hosts do not, they early on addressed such issues as zoning, taxation, insurance, and sanitary codes as they related to B&B. RSOs continue to seek solutions to a number of the problems common to all B&B hosts. Their greatest service to the many hosts who use them is their capacity for locating and screening guests.

In scope, RSOs can be national or international, state-wide, areawide, or limited to one major city. Many national RSOs have a special focus. Several large church organizations, the League of Women Voters, a number of college alumni associations, gays, teacher's associations, interracial groups, fifty-plus clubs, humanist groups, and many others have their own networks of B&Bs around the country. One RSO lists only houses certified on the National Historic Register. Some of these special focus RSOs have international, as well as domestic hosts on their lists.

Almost every state has one or more RSOs, so there should be one near you. Use the addresses in the Resource section (Part VI) to make inquiries of those RSOs that interest you. Before you make any commitments however, read on.

While some RSOs have been around a long time, many others are newcomers to the B&B scene. They are, in fact, springing up like the proverbial mushroom—paralleling the increase in B&B lodgings.

Because of this rapid RSO proliferation, there are wide differences in standards, experience and efficiency. While some RSOs don't last long, others have expanded rapidly, and the resultant diversity in expertise and business-like attitudes suggests that you, as a potential host, should shop around before committing yourself to one or more of these groups. Remember, most arrangements between the B&B and RSO are not informal, but are very specific, and may run for a year or longer. Some may be exclusive. Usually you will be signing a contract.

Try to judge how well the different RSOs meet your needs on the basis of the following criteria, which we discuss in the next few pages.

> Experience
> Operational structure
> Fee structure
> Advertising scope
> Exclusivity
> Standardization and availability
> What they offer you
> What obligations they impose

Experience. Find out how long each RSO you are considering has been in business. Presumably the more experienced they are, the more efficient and smooth will be their service both to you and the guest. Also, try to gauge how forthcoming they would be in putting this experience to work for you.

Variations in Structure. Operational structures for RSOs can differ in ways which can affect you, the host. Some RSOs are hosts themselves and have set up a reservation service in their area. They may or may not give themselves first shot at bookings. Some are not hosts but are strictly RSO operators. Some are a network of hosts in a specific area and handle their own organizational setup and publicity.

Some have toll-free numbers to call. Some are a computerized listing and referral service, with minimal screening. Some sell catalogs with descriptions of B&B homes (no addresses) and locations so that guests can self-select. Others control and carefully match the guests to host homes. Some require membership of guest, or host, or both, while others charge a single fee each time.

Some RSOs are quite large, others are small. Some operate only locally, others over a state, or nationally. Some let guests contact the host directly, others do not. Be certain the structure of whatever RSO you are considering is well-suited to your needs.

Fee Structure. The amount and structure of RSO fees vary. Some RSOs charge the host an annual membership fee of $20 to $50 or more. Others charge the host a commission—ten to twenty percent—for each booking they arrange. Some charge both fee and commission.

Usually guests pay either a membership fee or a service fee for each booking. The guest also may incur a phone bill for making the reservation. (Consider, in picking your RSO, that a guest who has paid a large RSO fee and then your lodging fee may be more demanding or have higher expectations. You, also, may feel more pressured knowing this.)

We have been solicited by several newly-formed RSOs and thought their fees rather high for what they offered compared to some of the more established ones. This may reflect a growing perception that there is money to be made in B&B. Do be wary of spending a lot and getting a little in return.

Note also that there are hidden fees in joining some RSOs. If, for instance, they require liability insurance and certain standardized furnishings, and if you are doing only occasional bookings, then you may not feel the extra costs are warranted.

Look for the fee structure that best fits your situation.

Advertising Scope. Establish whether the RSO(s) you are considering have other homes listed that are similar to yours. If so, they will be used to working with, publicizing and attracting guests for your kind of B&B. If not, they may not be the best for you. For example, if you live in a house and they handle mostly apartments, they may not be reaching—with their advertising focus—the kinds of guests who would match your home and fees. On the other hand, yours may be the kind of place an RSO might be glad to have for certain guests *because* yours is different from most of their listings. Ask about their listings.

The same holds for geographic area. An RSO's advertising is not going to do optimum work for you if it is not attracting enough guests who are looking for a B&B in your particular part of the country. However, many state or city RSOs are now networking with others across the country to broaden their contacts and draw from a larger pool of potential guests. A mix of localized and broader-based RSOs might get you the best results. Explore this.

Exclusivity. Exclusivity is like going steady—you are not supposed to go out with anyone else. With some RSOs you sign a contract to that effect. Exclusivity can be a useful tool to RSO operators, and a few of them insist upon it. From your point of view as a host, a high-volume business may mean that you need to deal with several RSOs. Unless your B&B is unusually attractive and well-situated, one RSO probably cannot provide enough bookings for you. Be cautious about signing an exclusive contract if you are interested in having more than just occasional guests.

Note also that almost all RSOs will expect that once a guest books with you through them, then each time that guest comes to you, he or she will owe the RSO a commission. If you feel uncomfortable about this, consider RSOs carefully. But, many, many hosts have repeat business through RSOs and are quite satisfied with this arrangement.

Standardization and Availability. The RSO you join will, understandably, ask you to meet their standards and to be available as a host with some degree of regularity.

Their standards simply may be that you provide a "reasonably clean" or "comfortable" home for B&B. Some require initial or periodic inspections of host homes. A few may have detailed specifications about room furnishings, smoke detectors, fire exits, lighting and breakfast. Some RSOs have a follow-up form for guests to complete after their stay in each B&B.

Many RSOs say that a complaint from a guest could drop a host from their list. Because some RSOs and most guidebook publishers now will accept a photograph and description of your home—they cannot personally inspect every B&B home beforehand—they use this warning as a way of cautioning hosts. It is unlikely that you would be dropped, but you should be aware of this possibility.

Explicit standards for furnishings are rare but could be a problem to some B&B hosts, especially for those individualists who prize the particular character of their home. RSOs understand that a major attraction of B&B is the distinctive character of each host home. Nevertheless it is easier for the RSOs to advertise knowing they can guarantee certain standardized accommodations. Thus, some RSOs prefer that all their listed homes be similar in certain minor ways. Explore this with the RSO you are considering before you find you have promised to do something you may not want to do in the way of setting up your guest room or breakfast table or dealing with fire precautions.

Host availability, within reasonable limits, is expected by RSOs. They try to work on an advanced planning schedule and need to know when you will be available. They will expect that you usually are receptive when they make a guest reservation, and if you keep refusing because it is inconvenient for you, you really are not living up to your agreement with them.

Weighing the Pros and Cons. Before deciding on one or more RSOs, use this checklist to weigh what you might get or give in your relationship with each one you are considering.

First, what you *might* get from an RSO:

Guests in the volume you desire.
Cheaper liability insurance (group).
Group purchasing of supplies (e.g., soap, towels, bed linens).
Publicity and advertising; printing, etc.
Advanced planning.
Information on zoning, insurance, fire laws, tax laws, etc.
Start-up information and on-site advice regarding your home; rate setting, etc.
Guest screening, handling of reservations and deposits, taking payments.

Up-to-date information regarding relevant new developments in the industry—maybe a newsletter.
A written contract spelling out all specifics.
Generally doing much of your legwork.

Second, what they *may* expect of you:

To set your rates for you.
A fee for their services.
A clean, attractive home.
A marketable home, which they may wish to inspect.
Conformity to certain standards of furnishings, cleanliness.
Exclusivity regarding other RSOs.
Commissions from return guests.
Mandatory liability coverage.
Advanced planning.
Being there, not too many turn-downs, host availability.
A written contract specifying the above.

Select the best RSOs for your needs. What might be ideal for one B&B host could be negative for another. You may have to experiment for a year or two before you get the ideal setup.

Listing in a Guidebook

Guidebook listings, like RSO listings, are particularly effective at bringing guests from farther afield compared to local contacts. They are a simple and inexpensive way to locate guests. A number of good guidebooks are available. Before listing in any, look them over in a library or bookstore and note their different styles and the areas they cover.

A comprehensive national guide for almost a decade has been Rundback's *Bed and Breakfast U.S.A.*, which has been on the best seller list for travel books the last few years. We have listed our B&B here and been pleased with the quality of guests it brought us. Another very comprehensive national guide, Lanier's *Complete Guide to Bed and Breakfast Inns and Guesthouses*, just came out last year, and has been generally well-received. Both these guides are updated annually.

There are a number of other excellent guidebooks, some national but most regional. Most give the host's name and address. A few give a description and general location of the B&B, but not the host's name and address. The host is contacted by guests via an RSO also listed in the guidebook. Some guidebooks are updated annually, some less frequently, and therefore are not immediately accessible to you. (A listing of guidebooks, with their addresses, is given in Part VI, the Resource section.)

Guidebook listings usually are organized by states. Based on whatever information you have provided them, they give a brief description of your home which distinguishes it from other listings. Thus, you control to some extent how you are described, and you can check the guidebook when it is published to confirm that both tone and facts are correct about your home, prices and policies.

In order to be listed you usually will be charged a fee, will have to fill out an application, describe your home, and will probably be asked to send a picture, and possibly be inspected. Most guidebook writers used to say they inspected all the places they listed, but this has become very difficult to do, as there are so many more B&B hosts.

Some guidebooks now put a stipulation on the bottom of their application form which says that they will drop you if you do not live up their standards. Their standards are usually only broadly defined (e.g., neat, clean), and apparently their judging you as unsuitable would be based on guest complaints. Some guides are now also including a mild disclaimer, perhaps to offset the vagueness of these "standards" and their enforcement. Do not be intimidated by doubts about whether you will pass muster and be listed. Write for an application and, if you have questions about standards, ask them.

Guidebooks Compared with RSOs. Your relationship with a guidebook—your inclusion therein—is a simpler matter than involvement with an RSO. Guidebook organizations do vary: some are membership organizations; some charge a listing fee; some are invitational and you cannot pay to be listed. Guidebook fees are usually paid annually and are cheaper than RSO fees, but they cannot offer you as many perks as do RSOs. Nor do guidebooks require as much from you.

Some guidebook publishers, such as the Tourist House Association of America (which issues *Bed and Breakfast USA*), offer group liability insurance at about $100 annually to their members. Other guidebook publishers note that they are exploring similar policies. Many also are talking about group life insurance policies for those who are listed in their guides. Like some RSOs, some guidebook writers also publish newsletters periodically. Unlike RSOs, guidebook publishers of course cannot screen guests, or make advance reservations.

Most guidebooks have wider circulation than do most individual RSOs, and many of the latter are now listing their organizations in the guidebooks. Guidebooks have no exclusivity stipulation, so you can easily list with as many as you wish. There is no written contract, although with some you do sign an application form or membership agreement. Guidebook writers, unlike most RSO operators, are not usually on hand to help with start-up information. In sum, your relationship with guidebooks will be much looser than with RSOs.

Making the decision whether to use an RSO or a guidebook or both will be based on your individual preferences and circumstances. RSOs are particularly appealing if your primary interest is guest screening or matching, if you do not want your address listed for public reading, if you do not want the trouble of locating guests and making reservations, if you do not want to collect money directly from your guests, and if you want to supplement your other marketing methods. RSOs may find you cheaper liability insurance than will a guidebook listing, and if you were going to buy it anyway, then this is a plus. Do remember that by listing with an RSO you will lose a little independence. Do not count on only one RSO always to fill your rooms. And keep in mind that the guest is paying more, and may expect more of you than guests you get through a guidebook.

The guidebook's listing may be cheaper and leave you more in control, but will also mean you will be on your own to a much greater extent—which may or may not appeal to you. Your name and address usually will be publicized, and you will have to do your own guest screening.

Ultimately, your personality and your individual circumstances: how independent you want to be; whether you are alone as a host; whether you live in the city or the country; how much you can spend; how selective you are; and how high a volume you are aiming for—will form your decision to use RSOs, guidebooks or both. Before signing or listing, use what you have learned from this chapter to help you get the deal that best suits you and will work to your best advantage for the least money.

PART V
Making Money

10
Setting Income Goals

How much money are you hoping to make from your B&B? Think this through carefully. A realistic income goal will be framed within the context of your home and location and energy level. Set initial goals you can meet without stress. Make them concrete and achievable. If you meet them easily, then redefine and enlarge them if you wish.

Meeting specific needs that are personally important to you is an intelligent and potentially satisfying way of defining initial B&B income goals. For example, to pay a substantial portion of your fuel bill with B&B income, or to redecorate your rooms. Or, to supplement your income or pension by so much per month, or to put so many dollars in your savings account annually, or to help with mortgage payments. You may need to replace income lost through family illness, or may want to bank B&B income for children's education or for special vacations. If your aims are realistic, you should be able to meet them and will know that the income is there as a cushion and a help.

Do not start out assuming you can live off your B&B income alone. This is not usually realistic and may never be so for your particular home or location. While it is true that B&B income is the main or only source of income for some hosts, this usually applies to large, well-established B&Bs. The average B&B is small.

A nationally-based B&B umbrella organization estimated, a year or so ago, B&B income topping off at about $2000 annually. Lots of hosts do make much more than that, and, of course, such estimates need annual updating because of rising prices. Several more recent estimates, made by knowledgeable B&B writers, gauged income at $10,000 annually or estimated average potential income, from just one room, at over $1000 monthly *if the B&B is properly marketed.* For most of us, the reality probably is somewhere in the middle of these two estimates. More to the point, the "bottom line," how much you actually do make each year from your B&B, will depend on the following:

- The time and physical energy you are willing to expend and the effort you want to make.
- Your home, its location, the number of rooms, and the rate you can charge.
- Your publicity efforts and the volume of business you attract.
- Optional services or items you can provide or sell.
- Your potential for expansion either of rooms or services.
- How carefully you watch expenses.
- Whether you take care to realize available tax savings.

The degree to which you seriously treat B&B as a business and try to reach the optimum in coordinating these various factors will make a great difference. The more casual you are about it, the less your potential or actual income.

11
Pricing Your Rooms

How do you arrive at an appropriate price for your guest room—a rate that is competitive, offers good value to the guest, and is the most productive for you, the host? There are several elements to be considered.

Some of you, of course, will feel from the outset quite confident about what you want to charge, especially if you have other B&Bs in your area to use as a yardstick. Some of you even may be able to consult with other B&B hosts, or, if you are considering listing with an RSO (reservation service organization), they may help you set your rate. However, it is wise to develop your own sense of what your room(s) is worth, rather than relying only on the advice of others, especially if they are not totally disinterested parties.

For those of you who are doing it on your own and are confused about pricing, the following pages give a detailed plan for rate-setting. The essence of the procedure is to find your approximate basic rate, discount it from the comparable hotel or motel rate, and then add on to it for any additional features your home has, or subtract for certain drawbacks. If you are comparing yourself only to B&Bs you do not need to discount this way, but should raise or lower your fee in accordance with features your B&B does or does not have.

Carefully feel your way into setting your rates the first year. Thereafter you may wish to raise or lower them because of what you have learned. The initial rate set, however, should be as close as you can come to the best rate for your particular situation.

Finding Your Basic Category

Your first step, obviously, is to research the competition. Find out the range of prices for hotels, motels, other B&Bs, guest houses, hostels and Ys in your area. Do this by phoning or visiting them yourself, talking to others who have used them, or checking out guidebooks which list lodgings for your area. It is most helpful to actually see the various rooms yourself. If you live in a rural area or smaller town, you may have to sample from a broad area to get enough information to make your comparisons.

If you are not too many miles from a major tourist attraction, check out B&B and hotel or motel listings for places closer to that attraction. Judge from these rates if you can afford to advertise yourself as a cheaper alternative to the higher rate travelers are paying to be near at hand. Become familiar with what is being offered, and at what price, in or near your area, and beyond, if it will be helpful.

When researching rates, get specific details. The comparisons you make also will be specific. Find out rates for singles and doubles, for double and twin beds, and for cots for extra persons; for shared or private bath, children over and under twelve, rates in and out of season, or daily or weekly, and for suites with kitchens. Find out about discounts for senior citizens, and about special features like pools or television, which most motels have but most B&Bs may not. In order to be competitive, you must define exactly what you are competing with.

For the near future, at least, the competition you are comparing your B&B with is more likely to be composed of hotels and motels rather than B&Bs. As you start researching these motels and hotels, or checking out guidebooks, you will see that there are various classes of accommodations available. Different places label these classes by different names. They generally can be lumped into the following categories:

1. Modest; economy; extremely reasonable (i.e., clean and functional, perhaps not as well located or embellished).
2. Average; moderate; reasonable (i.e., better than #1, plus maybe an attractive or unusual feature).
3. Luxury; deluxe; exceptional (i.e., better than #2, with several attractive features and services).
4. Unusual; superior; four-star (i.e., tops, really posh, elegant, unusual).

You should be able to judge *approximately* which category you fit into. The majority of B&Bs probably fall into the second. Take a look at your home. You have seen what local motel accommodations look like. Compare, and place yourself roughly in category one, two, three or four. Now figure, for example, what the average rate is in your area for a double room in each of these categories. (Hotel and motel rates may be more in line with each other for each category; B&B rates probably vary more from each other because they are less standardized.)

To find your B&B base rate, you usually should discount your B&B somewhat from the motel or hotel rate. B&Bs falling into category one could be discounted up to as much as half of the average rate for similar rooms in local motels; those in the second category discounted one-quarter to one-third. Those in category three will be equal to or higher than the motel price, because at this point they are as attractive as, or possibly preferable to the motels. The very top, category four, will be highly priced on its own special merits and have perhaps no apparent relationship to other local accommodations. You have now done the first step in pricing by working out a rough basic rate.

Do not neglect looking over the hotel/motel competition just because you have been lucky enough to be able to compare your rate with a number of other B&Bs. Check out some of the former to assure yourself that you truly are providing an affordable, reasonable alternative to more conventional lodgings in the area.

Of course, if you were able to find a number of B&Bs in your area, then you have had a more specific standard to go by. Presumably the other B&Bs have already discounted themselves from the hotel/motel rates, and have now created their own rate scale for B&Bs in the area, just by being there. Even so, you still should follow the steps on the next pages and adjust your rate by comparing your B&B to the others on the various features and services we note.

Adjusting for Location

The local rates you have been researching will reflect the value already set by other hosts and guests in the particular location you share. If yours is a very popular area, the rates will be higher. If it is less popular, the rates will be lower, especially if you have sampled over a broad geographic area where lodgings are scattered rather than concentrated. However, *where* you are within this geographic area can further influence your rate. For example, if you are in the country, are you very close to the major tourist attraction? Or, are you in the heart of a city, near the action? Are you very close to a superhighway or a great restaurant? Rate your location within the area itself. If the location is better than, or less good than average for your area, add or subtract $2-4 accordingly.

Unusual Features

Now tally bonuses, the unusual features of your B&B. Look at the list below and see if any of these apply to your home. Each adds to the rate you can charge for your B&B.

Pool or pond (swimming or skating).
Historic or old (turn-of-the-century or older) house.
Striking contemporary house or apartment.
Waterfall.
Views.
Good bird-watching or nature walks.
Furnished with antiques.
Furnished with modern art (original paintings) and furniture.
Tennis.
Horseback riding.
Farm animals.
Grounds for walking, picnicking or riding.
Fireplace in guest room.
Library or conference room.
Living or sitting room with piano or fireplace or TV.
Patio or balcony or porch or deck.
Sunporch or solarium.
Barbecue grill and picnic tables.
Fishing from beach or in trout stream or lake.
Boats/rowing/sailing.
Ice skating and cross-country skiing or nearby access to these.

If you have an historic old or newer home as noted above, add $4-8 to the base price you arrived at for your category. Tote up any of the other things on the list which apply to you and add approximately another $1-2, for each one, to your base price.

Baths and Breakfasts

If you have more than four persons sharing a bath, you should lower your base price $1-2, and if you offer a private bath with the room you should raise it by $1-3.

Make sure the cost of breakfast is reflected in your rate. Presumably, most of the places you have been checking out will be motels and hotels, so they will not be offering breakfast—although it is surprising how many large motels now display big Bed and Breakfast signs even though they are not really B&Bs.

One cannot serve a decent continental breakfast (coffee, toast or muffin, juice, jam, butter, sugar and cream) for less than $1.25-$1.50 including time and materials. Figure breakfast for two at about $2.50, and if you are offering more, such as fresh fruit or a full breakfast, or if you're doing some really sensational breakfast offering, charge for it separately or make sure it is reflected in your room rate.

Other Variations on Basic Rates

Singles should never be lowered to as little as half of doubles. They cost very close to the same amount in terms of laundry, cleaning, and electricity—fewer towels and less breakfast being the major differences. So 10%, 15% or maybe 20% off the rate for doubles is reasonable.

If you have an extra person, whether child or adult, and put in a crib or cot, charge $7-10 extra. You will still have extra work, and extra laundry and food. Be very careful not to underprice here, as this costs more than you might think.

Some hosts will lower the rate slightly if one family occupies two rooms, with adults in one room and their children in a second room. This seems unfair to the host since the laundry and cleaning involved are the same, but you may wish to give such an option to families. Also, some hosts have a "two-night minimum" policy and will add a surcharge for one-night stays.

You may also wish to give weekly or seasonal discounts, or discounts to senior citizens. Check out your competition and see what they are doing before you decide. Discounts are tricky with B&B. If you are already charging a very reasonable rate, make sure you really can afford the discount—it may be that you cannot. Many B&Bs are so reasonable that they do not offer discounts.

Additional Features and Services

You must decide if you want to charge separately for additional features and services or include them in your rate by raising it.

Additional features do not always have the value of the bonuses or unusual features already noted, and guests may seldom utilize them. But you certainly can add $1-2 for them in your rate as, for example:

King-sized bed
Guest refrigerator
Waterbed
Hot tub
Complimentary fruit or wine in the room
Television or phone in the room

You may also be offering an unusual breakfast; make sure its ingredients are accounted for in the rate.

Whether you want to charge separately or absorb into your rate the use of laundry, refrigerator, kitchen, iron, or bicycles may depend on how much you find that people actually use them. Rather you might charge for them as they are used, just as you might charge separately for other special services such as airport pickup, tourist information, ticket reservations, and local tours. In the next section we will discuss charging for special services. The decision we are discussing here is whether to charge separately for such services or add them to your room rate.

Testing Your Rate

Forty dollars is the current estimated average price of a B&B room in season. This figure has appeared in a number of recent articles, including the *New York Times* "Real Estate Section." A perusal of the guidebooks will show the range around this average: room rates of $20 to $145. Presumably, they will continue to go up. Meantime, what have you come up with for your own room? By now you should have tallied up all your pluses and minuses and arrived at some fairly good idea of what your room(s) is worth. Whatever that sum is, try it for a while.

During the trial period, average out your costs for laundry, breakfast, cleaning materials, heat, electricity and your time—all that goes into your B&B expenses—to confirm that you are staying well ahead of your operating costs with whatever rate you set. You should be seeing a profit. If you are not you must rethink your fees.

They are not written in stone, so if adjustment is necessary from time to time, do it. Costs will continue to rise. You will learn better what you are spending for advertising and what is the value of your own time. You will soon know if you are providing too much of a bargain or pricing yourself out of the volume of business you would like to do.

If people keep telling you it's a bargain, then it is and you should raise it a few dollars. Don't be shy about it. But don't be greedy, either, and push for all that the traffic will bear and more. If you start getting grumbles and complaints you've gone too far. Remember that lower rates ultimately can mean more income through more volume, and that recommendations and repeat business from satisfied guests earn you a lot of good publicity, while saving time and expense.

If you consider contracting with an RSO, and they set your rates, be sure you are comfortable with the figure they suggest. Rely on your own sense of what is right for you—and what is locally competitive—to confirm that the rate is appropriate. Neither should you guarantee your rate, as some guidebooks may request, unless you are sure it is set high enough that you will still be making an adequate profit through the whole year until the guidebook is updated.

12
Expenses and Savings

Do not spend money on your B&B without good reason or planning. Before incurring an expense, review your priorities. Is the projected expense vital to your income and other goals, or can it wait? Try to avoid impulsive expenditures.

Where You Will Spend Money

You will have four major categories of expenses:

Start-up
Promotional
Operating
Maintenance

They will occur in approximately that order and later overlap, except for start-up expenses, which eventually become maintenance expenses.

Start-up includes: whatever you do to decorate (e.g., paint, curtains, wallpaper); what you do to make your place more functional (e.g., towel rack, guest book, soap dish, hall night light, smoke detector), and what you do to furnish it (e.g., towels, sheets, reading lamps).

Promotional expenses could include: printing of business cards or brochures, paper, stamps, envelopes, telephone calls, directory listing fee, rubber stamp, guidebook or RSO listing fee, car mileage, membership in a chamber of commerce.

Operating expenses could include: electricity, gas, oil, food, cleaning help and equipment and materials, laundry, soap, light bulbs, and, possibly, liability insurance.

Maintenance can include: retouching paint, replacing worn towels or sheets, repainting, replacing shades, keeping yard mowed and neater than you may have done before, or walks shovelled and snow-free.

Start-up expenses obviously are a one-time expense. Operating and maintenance expenses will increase as your volume increases. Promotional expenses may or may not increase as time passes, depending on the methods you use. Your labor is also a part of all of these things. Realistically assess the time you are putting in to make sure you are getting adequate recompense. Whatever you spend, keep complete records.

Where You Can Save Money

If yours is to be a high-volume business with a steady stream of guests, then you will have more gross expenses, but you should have a greater net profit as well.

If it is to be a minimal operation—a guest once in a while—watch your expenses too. If you go all-out on those few occasions when you have weekend B&B guests, then your motivation should be to show off your house, or to find new bridge partners, because you won't make much money—unless, of course, your house is very special and the rate at a premium.

In order to maximize your profit, watch expenses as closely as you would in any other kind of business, and do not over-prepare, over-promote, or over-host.

Over-preparing. A common pitfall for new B&B hosts is that because they are charging people for staying in their own home they feel unsure or even a bit self-conscious about what they have to offer and what they have to do to make their home acceptable as a place people will pay to stay in. You must deal with your feelings about this before you ready your home for B&B. Do not incur unnecessary expenses because of this uncertainty. Concerns about "image" should not push you into over-preparing on decorating, extras, breakfast, and so on. Think about who and what you are, your life style and what is comfortable to you, then do your preparation affordably.

Further, make sure of your priorities and needs. Take one step at a time, as you learn. Do not resurface the driveway and paint the house in getting ready. After you have run a B&B for a while, you may feel that a new showerhead is more important than new paint. Your perception of priorities will change with experience.

Always try to make do as much as possible with what you already have. B&Bs are not supposed to be alike, and using your own things will put your individual touch on it. If the room is clean, attractive and functional, it should do for Bed and Breakfast. We would suggest that you use much of your start-up money, if you can spend some, more towards making your B&B functional than making it highly decorative. A smooth experience for the guest is a must; extra adornments can come later.

Over-promoting. Do not order expensive letterhead, receipt books, reservation and billing materials, and imprinted items just to look good. Have confidence in yourself. Start inexpensively. Buy a rubber stamp instead. You can use it for letterheads, return addresses, receipts, and check endorsements; rubber stamps look more businesslike than does handwriting.

If you do have a brochure printed, write it yourself. Get someone you know to make a line drawing of your house. Have the printer do your layout only if he does not charge extra for it. Otherwise, try to get someone you know to do it, or do it yourself following the examples given in Chapter 8 and adapting them to your particular needs. Do not put material needing annual updating and reprinting—such as room rates—into the brochure itself. Save yourself later printing bills.

Do not over-advertise. Think carefully before you spend advertising dollars. Do not list with several RSOs or guidebooks unless you can see an obvious payoff; weigh the relative merits of each, and choose one or two.

Do not overspend out of nervousness. If you do not have many guests the first year, it will pick up—if you are doing things right—and you will do two to three times your first year's business the second year. By then you will have some sense of where it might be helpful to spend more money on advertising. And, if you join an RSO (Reservation Service Organization), get them to do some of the promotion for you. (See Chapter 9.) Be prepared to start slowly until you can better judge where publicity dollars might pay off.

Over-hosting. It is fun and easy to be the generous host, but don't get carried away. Balance gracious generosity with common sense. Otherwise, as you overdo free drinks, food, phone and so on, you cut into your profit. Extras are a nice gesture to guests who return or who send others to you, or with whom you have become friends, but think through your policy on extras before trapping yourself into spontaneous over-hosting.

Offer the guests what they should expect from your brochure or guide listing or from other publicity; balance the extras by making sure they are covered in your fee. Be realistic about both your costs and the kinds of expectations you want to create in your guests. Remember that they may come back or send other guests. Extras could become something guests expect, without your having intended it. We are not suggesting that you never "overhost." Don't be "mean." If you enjoy generous hosting, do it. Just be sure you want to before you act.

Laundry and Cleaning. Laundry is one of your major expenditures. If you have your own washer-drier, you will save significantly by doing your B&B laundry yourself. If you do not have a machine, you might set buying one as a goal of your B&B income and then use it as a tax deduction. If you take your laundry to the local laundromat, ask for a discount since you are a local small business. Or, ask one of your neighbors if they will do laundry for you at less than laundromat rates. Give serious thought to the cheapest way to do your laundry.

Cleaning usually can be done by the B&B host, unless there is a very heavy volume of business. If you need help, perhaps you can pay someone in the neighborhood to help you make beds and do the vacuuming. If you do hire help, be organized and ready so you get the best use of their time and your money. Always buy your laundry detergents and cleaning supplies when there are sales. Stock up when the price is low.

Food. Food is another consistent expenditure. Many of the things you serve for breakfast can be bought more cheaply when they are on sale, and then frozen for later use. Bread, English muffins, donuts and orange juice are obvious examples. Save money on breakfast, but still make a good impression by baking or making something yourself. Home-baking goes over well with guests.

While you must make sure the cost is reflected in your room rate, breakfast is a very special part of B&B and should not be skimped on. Make sure it pays for itself, but do serve a generous and pleasing breakfast.

Utility and Telephone Bills. We have found that B&B guests do not make an appreciable difference in our utility costs, but this might be different for B&B hosts with all-electric or air-conditioned homes. Telephone costs always should be carefully monitored, as they could make a difference. Do not accept collect calls. Do not offer to call back on long distance calls. Write instead. Make your telephone available to your guests, but have it clearly understood that they must pay for toll calls. Be sure to keep the phone log that is noted in Chapter 5. If you have an answering machine, make it clear on your recording that you will confirm reservations by mail only. Offer to send a brochure if callers leave their name and address. Tell them if time is short to call again at a specific time when you will be in. Do not use the phone yourself if the mail will serve as well. Avoid last-minute situations where you have to phone because the mails are too slow. If you are not careful about your phone use, it will nibble away at your profits.

Breakage. If a guest inadvertently breaks something, how you handle the situation will depend on the item, the amount, and on you. You may want to ask them to pay for it, or to let it go, depending on the circumstances. Or, your insurance may cover it.

We have never had any breakage other than a few pieces of molding chipped by a suitcase or other heavy item hitting it. But if you have expensive breakage, do not be shy about being recompensed by the guest. They may have insurance which covers such a situation. Use your common sense and do not leave objects which have great sentimental value, or are irreplaceable, in your guest rooms.

No-Shows. Try not to lose money on people who do not show up. Be business-like about getting deposits, make your refund policy clear, and do not be hesitant about sticking to it. Change this procedure only if you think the circumstances are so very unusual that they warrant an exception.

In your brochure or your telephone conversation with potential guests, state clearly your refund policy on deposits. For instance, you may refund the deposit if you are given one or two weeks, or ten days notice. Or you may say that you will return the deposit if you rent the room. Or you may say that you will not return the deposit because you have already turned away someone when you thought you were fully booked. We have returned deposits as long as we did not turn down another booking before we knew of the cancellation of the first one. Whatever policy you decide on, make it clear and stick to it.

If, as frequently happens, someone calls the night before and you do not have time to get a deposit from them, tell them they must be there by such and such a time or they have the choice of reconfirming, or losing the booking if you get another inquiry. Finally, if you have a credit card affiliation, no-shows can be guarded against via credit card by asking for their credit card number when the reservation is taken.

Never be too timid to keep the deposit of people who did not show up. One or two no-show occurrences will convince you how expensive and disappointing it is. Be up-front with your deposit policy and expect potential guests to be the same about it. Most of the time they will be. We have found that if we are clear and firm about deposit refunds we seldom have problems with no-shows.

Tax Savings. It has already been noted, in Chapter 4, how you can realize tax savings in your B&B operation with deductions, depreciation, and, in special cases, tax credits. Documentation is absolutely necessary. You will not get these tax savings unless you keep good records—dates, amounts, purposes of expenditures. Do not fall behind in keeping your records and then waste time trying to reconstruct, always be up-to-date.

13
Expanding Your Income Potential

Possible ways to maximize income include increasing bookings, expanding services and retailing items relevant to your B&B or your locality. Also, you might consider establishing your own reservation service organization for your area. Any or all of these things could increase your income.

Another Room, or Renting Your Unhosted Apartment

Do you have another room that you could make available if necessary? Perhaps it is now used as a sewing room or junk room. Or, it may be the one that you usually use yourself, but perhaps you can sleep somewhere else once in a while. This is a bother, but it could double your income. The *Wall Street Journal,* in a recent story on Bed and Breakfast, described one B&B where the host slept on his terrace and rented his own bedroom during the summer months.

Couples and families frequently travel together, so that three to six persons in a party are not uncommon, and if you have only one room, you may have to turn guests away because you cannot accommodate them all. Think about a back-up second room you could use in such cases. Since you probably will not rent it as much, you will not have to keep it as well prepared, but you will have to make some concessions to how you use it in order to have it fairly ready.

Another alternative, if you are away yourself, is to rent your apartment. You can charge more for an unhosted apartment than you can if you are there sharing it with the guest. This kind of rental usually is done through an RSO so that the guest is screened before coming into your unoccupied apartment.

More Bookings

The more you publicize and the more guests you have, the more bookings you will get. Repetition of advertising, and guest referrals, bring in more people and spread the word more broadly. Never allow promotional efforts to slacken.

Let previous guests as well as potential new guests know of new rooms or services available. Think about changing some of your policies, such as allowing hunters, smokers, guests with pets. Offer discounts for seasonal events and special weekend packages. Drum up business in new ways.

Extra Services

Offer extra services and either charge separately for them or raise your fee to cover them, depending on whether everyone, or only selected guests will use them. Examples are:

Evening cocktails
Airport or railroad pickup
Making reservations for dinner, car, theatre, or concert
Doing laundry
Renting out bicycles or sports equipment
Baby or pet sitting

Guided tours are in demand in the city—or anywhere when people want to see a lot in a short time. Box lunches are popular with hikers, bicyclers and outdoor concert-goers.

Selling Related Items

Some B&B hosts have a gift shop on or adjacent to their premises. Others simply display items for sale in their hall or dining room. These can include tourist information kits you have put together yourself (lists of shopping places, current events, local attractions with dates and hours and directions to reach them); a guidebook of your area; post cards; T-shirts; local products (e.g., maple syrup, sea shells) and souvenirs. Many B&B guidebook publishers will give you commissions on sales of their books, or sell you their publications at a discount for resale. (See Resource section, Part VI.)

B&B Guidebooks for Your Area

You might put together a B&B guidebook for your own area if there are enough—say, eight or more—lodgings or inns available. You can charge other B&B hosts a fee for a guidebook listing and also sell advertising space to local businesses. If you have started your own back-up network (see Chapter 5) it could be the basis for your guidebook. Local stores and other B&B hosts might buy the guide for resale. If you print a guidebook, perhaps your first edition should be a photocopy or mimeographed job, with stapled binding, to keep costs down. Watch production costs or you will not make a profit.

Update Your Fee

Rethink your fee and update it periodically. Make sure it always reflects the new services you have instituted or expenses you have incurred due to inflation or to improvements in your B&B. A fee should not be static; it needs annual or semi-annual reevaluation.

Starting an Inn

If you want to expand in a big way, then you might seriously consider a B&B inn, or even an inn offering full meal service. A small, home-based B&B is good training ground for such a venture. It gives you a chance to see how you react to new people, and to dealing with all sorts of unanticipated, small problems around the house or with the hired help or your guests. You learn how to get breakfast organized and on the table quickly; what the area's seasonal flow is; where the costs are, and where advertising is best used. Without having made the expensive commitments of inn-keeping, you will have a track-record to present to your bank if you need financing in order to expand.

A B&B inn or a country inn serving meals will be larger and less homey, by necessity, than a small B&B. You probably cannot sustain quite the same one-to-one hospitality with so many more guests. Nor will you have the same flexibility in, for example, declining guests on those weekends when you don't want to be a host. You will have more responsibilities, with little let-up except perhaps a seasonal rest. Innkeeping is hard work and not to be undertaken lightly.

On the other hand, the potential certainly exists for making substantially more than you can with a home-based B&B. Besides having more rooms, inns have more uses as well. For example, they are becoming popular as conference centers. They are more interesting places than motels, and offer more privacy for business meetings. Inns also have more promotional possibilities. Because they are larger, the innkeeper can hold "events" at the inn for large numbers of people. They are usually ideal for wedding receptions.

At least one book is available on starting a country inn which serves meals. And, at this writing there are a number of persons who make a business of coaching people about, or actually through the whole process of, buying and operating a country inn. Some of the recently established B&B newsletters have listed upcoming classes or seminars about innkeeping. (See Resource section, Part VI.)

Starting Your Own Reservation Service Organization

Discussed in Chapter 9 were the implications for you, the individual B&B host, of joining an RSO. In this section the perspective is just the opposite: we explore the possibility of running your *own* booking agency.

Advantages and Disadvantages. Operating an RSO is more complicated than running an individual B&B. A greater commitment of time is needed, and you must persist over a long enough period to build up the pool of hosts necessary to raise your profit potential. The advantages of having your own booking agency are first, that you have the initial contact with the prospective guest, and therefore the first chance to rent your own B&B if you wish. Second, if you cannot take a guest yourself, you can receive a commission or membership fee from another host for the referral.

The disadvantages are that you will have heavier responsibilities, not only for yourself, but for others. You will be screening and locating hosts and guests; setting standards and maybe rates for others; taking reservations; matching host and guest; advising hosts and doing publicity.

To do all this with authority, you must plan well beforehand. Use the information in this book to help you pick hosts, screen guests, do publicity, rate homes, and so on. For in-the-field advice, however, it might be helpful to seek out a larger RSO which covers a broad area, including yours. They might counsel you about your own RSO if they are interested in networking with you. Check the Resource section, (Part VI) for RSOs near you and contact a few with this in mind.

Expenses. As an RSO operator your expenses will be more than they were as a B&B host. You will have long-distance telephone calls and will need letterhead, lots of file cards, and possibly an answering machine. Postage, advertising and car mileage could be major expenses. You will have legal fees and greater need of an accountant. Also, if you are successful you may need to hire help with clerical work.

Registering a Name. Whether you call your group a booking agency, a referral service, a reservation service organization, or something else, give it a specific name. This name should convey coverage of your city, area, county—wherever you are aiming— and be so distinctive that it cannot be easily confused with another. (Refer to the Resource section to see the kinds of names others give their RSOs.) Register this name under business registrations, probably with the county clerk in your county. Usually there will be a list of all business names already registered there. Make sure that yours does not duplicate someone else's; that could invalidate your registration.

Locating Hosts. It is better to start small than to overstep your capabilities. Begin locally. If you have already developed some sort of overflow network (see Chapter 5), you may be able to use it as the nucleus for your RSO, unless you personally find it awkward to ask these people for a commission when you have been in the habit of informally referring guests back and forth to each other.

Word-of-mouth is one way to find potential hosts. Advertising is another method. Still another is to search guidebooks for already existing B&Bs in your area. And ask at the chamber of commerce;

we found that potential hosts call there to advise of their availability. Look in telephone books; watch for business cards on bulletin boards. Then call any possibilities and see if they are interested in your RSO.

Contact B&Bs in a broad area around you and announce that you are running an informational meeting for actual or potential B&B hosts. Your chamber of commerce or community college might welcome your giving such a seminar at no cost. We have seen just such interest in our area.

Remember that you are going to advertise to find guests, and send them to hosts who are going to pay you for the referral, so select prospective hosts with this in mind. You and the host both will be protected by a contract, but it is still better to work with reasonable, relaxed people who seem likely to deal with you in a professional manner.

It can be fun to meet potential hosts and to see their homes. If you are a good judge of people, you will be selecting the same kinds of hosts we have emphasized; they will be comfortable meeting others, glad to have guests in their homes and will be well-prepared. Just because you think their house is great for B&B, don't take on people who might be uneasy as hosts. Even with a contract between you, there could be problems.

Sometimes you may find people who are not really suited—or their homes are not suited—to B&B, but who want to try anyway. Be firm about screening out inappropriate hosts—people who because of their space, location, homes or personalities, you judge would not work out well. Finding hosts is a slow process, and it should be. Do not expect to do it rapidly, or you may find yourself regretting an impulsive decision. Solid RSOs have taken some years to establish.

Locating, Screening and Matching Guests. Locating guests will mean using the same methods we have already discussed. As an RSO operator, however, you will have to do more advertising to find guests than you did as a single B&B host, since you need a much greater volume of guests. And, unless you are going to sell your host list to potential guests rather than make reservations for them, you also will have the added responsibility of screening guests and sometimes matching them with hosts.

You will have to decide how and how much you want to screen and match. To do either you will need at least a minimal information sheet on guests. Most information sheets are fairly detailed.

At the least always get relevant personal information:

Name
Address
Telephone number
Work address and telephone number
Number of people in the party
Ages of children
Specific arrival and departure dates and estimated time of
   arrival

You may wish to get much more information: driver's license number; a credit card number; personal references. Some RSOs even ask for a photograph of the guest and send it along to the host. If you think your hosts are this demanding, or that the homes need this much "security" in terms of screening, you will protect yourself by adopting rigorous screening methods. If you are going to try to match guests with hosts, then you will need more personal information about both of them. Many times, however, a reservation simply may resolve itself into what host in the desired area has a vacancy at the time required.

Some standard guest questions you might ask to help match host and guest are:

> The purpose of the trip.
> What they particularly want to be close to.
> Whether they have strong preferences about single or double beds, no pets, no smoking, no drinking.
> Whether they have allergies that would affect where they stayed.
> Whether they have to be near public transportation or will they have a car or will they need host pick-up.
> Whether they are handicapped in any way so that something such as stairs would be a problem.
> Whether they want a shared bath and continental breakfast or a private bath and full breakfast.

Any comments they make about the kind of place they would prefer could be helpful to you. If you ask for their preferences, don't promise to meet them unless you know absolutely that you can deliver; just say you'll try. Or, if you cannot deliver and know you cannot, say so at the outset.

Some RSOs print a descriptive brochure giving examples of their host homes. Some also give names and addresses, and guests make their own contracts. Again, the choice is yours.

Defining your Organization. Define how your organization is to work. Set standards to which all involved will be expected to adhere. First, for the host homes, will be certain standards of cleanliness and comfort and minimum breakfast. What these standards of cleanliness and comfort are must be clearly defined by you and discussed with the host. The host must agree to be consistent in upholding these standards, and you should be prepared to check from time to time to see that they are.

Whether you wish to check with guests yourself, or have them fill out a rating sheet at the end of their stay is your decision. RSO and guidebook writers vary in whether and how often they make visits to every home they list. It is not possible for writers of the larger guidebooks to visit all host homes. They may rely on guest complaints to let them know whether to continue listing. Most RSO operators visit most of their host homes. It would be helpful to do so if you can.

You are entitled to evaluate host homes in terms of whether they are keeping their part of the contract. Be careful not to make harsh or unreasonable standards. To try to keep standards exactly the same for every host home—in terms of where furniture should be placed, or lamps, or whatever—may not always be feasible. Hosts should be able to live comfortably within the "letter of the law" in terms of whatever your contract says. Also, the host should be fairly available to you, either at home or at work. If a host is going to be away, you should be advised beforehand.

The same is true of your guests. You should be able, politely, to make it clear to them that they are staying in someone's private home, with their prized personal possessions, and that they, the guests, should act accordingly. Don't make a lecture out of it; but your guest membership contract, or brochure, or commission form, should remind them of this.

Let guests know if you want feedback. It will be important to keep a fair balance between guest and host in terms of rights and responsibilities. If, because they are paying a commission, you think that the guest is always right, you could eventually alienate some of your host homes.

All these details, as well as the way in which payment is to be made, should be in the contract you sign with host or guest. It should note what your responsibilities are and what you are getting in return, and should do the same for host and guest. Be careful not to imply in the host contract that you will supply a large quantity of guests. You probably will not be able to do so unless their location and home are exceptionally good and you have ways of consistently locating a large number of guests.

Contracts of course, should be signed by both of you, and the dollar or percentage amounts being paid in membership or commissions should be clearly set forth. What you will do to screen, to carry out publicity and to arrange conditions for payment (cash, checks, credit cards; beforehand, upon arrival, upon departure) must be stated. You should have a lawyer help design this contract.

For screening and warranting the host home, ask your lawyer if having a disclaimer might be wise. Further, you will be giving your hosts information and advice and they will be asking you about local rules and regulations, so clear with your lawyer whatever you are going to do in this regard.

You are taking on the responsibility for knowing state, local and federal regulations; zoning, tax and health laws, as they relate to your B&B network and the individual hosts. You may find it simpler to start in one city or county in order to learn to deal with one set of statutes or regulations. Protect yourelf by being well-informed on all matters relevant to you and your hosts.

Again, we suggest that networking with an experienced RSO could be very helpful with these matters. Many RSOs now are networking around the country to expand their coverage. It also might be helpful to join one or more of the professional information groups, such as American Bed and Breakfast Association, which publish monthly newsletters about new developments and deal with problems similar to those experienced by all RSO operators.

Epilogue:
Some Thoughts for
Serious B&B Hosts

Until relatively recently, individual B&B hosts were scattered around the country and had little or no contact with each other. Nor did they have specific mechanisms for developing an overview of B&B. With the growth in numbers of hosts, guidebooks and reservation service organizations, the individual B&B host is becoming aware that he or she is only one of an increasing number. Nevertheless, it still is not the norm to find individual hosts having consistent and organized contacts with many other hosts.

Because each RSO is more broadly organized then each individual host, RSOs have been much quicker than hosts to see the advantages of interconnecting with other RSOs and establishing networks or trade associations in order to exchange information or lobby for their interests. The result of this is that as the world of B&B expands, it tends to be the RSOs, not the individual hosts, who are more influential in shaping the image of what is now being called the "B&B industry," and defining and dealing with common concerns.

From their vantage point, RSOs see that B&B is growing into a larger and larger segment within the travel industry, and they feel that it should be handled more as are other accommodations. Yet, their intercommunication between networks, computer processing of reservations, toll-free numbers, and suggestions about classifying host homes into standardized, different levels of accommodations, all to some extent negate the homey, intimate image that so many of the travelling public have of B&Bs. Some RSOs also would like to "improve" the image of B&B beyond that of the cheap alternative to motels that some of the travelling public perceives.

On the other hand, RSOs are aware that television, newspapers and magazines do a disservice to the average B&B host when they stress the very unusual, posh, select, expensive places in their coverage of B&B. Indeed, RSO concerns for and perceptions about B&B are not always so different from those of many B&B hosts. The differences may more often lie in how solutions are defined or approached. But without more input from individual hosts, these solutions may reflect only the RSO point-of-view.

Hosts should recognize that many of the things RSOs are working for also could be helpful to the individual host, and that hosts would be wise to adopt similar tactics. Working under the aegis of large host associations would standardize practices and procedures so that there would be more consistency in how B&Bs operate: in their deposit and refund policies; their policing of both RSOs and hosts; professionalism, integrity, living up to standards, etc. All things which might clarify B&B and make it even more attractive to travellers.

Intercommunication between RSO and host associations also would facilitate information flow by making it easy to pool area or state-wide information on insurance, zoning, sales tax, licensing, health codes—all the things which are so hard to pin down—making it available, and keeping it updated, via computer systems or newsletters within host or RSO or joint associations.

Since it is primarily RSO organizations which are trying to deal in a more organized way with the issues that arise as B&B grows—issues affecting hosts and guests as well as RSOs—B&B hosts are missing an opportunity in not forming their own association in each locality or state. They need to have their own voices heard, to have their own input into policy decisions. Having their own associations involved in these processes would help them in the very tricky task of trying to keep their individuality while at the same time establishing some standards which might make B&B less confusing to travellers. Many hosts have the competence and the time to organize B&B hosts in their own states. It would better reflect the realities of the B&B "industry" over the next few years if hosts had equal weight with RSOs in dealing with some of the situations that are occurring on a general basis as B&B expands. Serious B&B hosts should start working on this now. Think about your own area and state. Perhaps networking with other hosts is easier than you think. And, if you don't do it, someone else will, without your input. Nothing seems to stand still with Bed and Breakfast.

PART VI
Resource File/
Where to Write

Within these files are listed titles, names, addresses and telephone numbers of various persons, groups or organizations you may need to contact in order to set up your B&B. These lists were updated as of the time this book went to press, and, the lists are as comprehensive as possible. However, organizations come into or go out of business with some rapidity, or they move, or they change their titles or phone numbers. Therefore, you may, when using these files, find here and there some deviation from the information listed.

Guidebooks to List In

This Resource File lists established guidebooks having national or regional listings. As we have noted in Chapter 9, fees vary for listing, and some are by invitation only. Write to those which are applicable to your geographic area and inquire. Be sure to find out how often they are updated or how often they publish a supplement: that is, how soon you can be listed.

Bed & Breakfast U.S.A., by Betty Rundback and Nancy Kramer.
Tourist House Association
R.D. 2, Box 355A
Greentown, PA 18426

The Complete Guide to Bed & Breakfasts, Inns and Guesthouses, by
   Pamela Lanier.
The Complete Guide to Bed & Breakfasts, Inns and Guesthouses
P.O. Box 20467
Oakland, CA 94620-0467

Bed & Breakfast Hostlist, compiled by
American Bed & Breakfast Association
P.O. Box 23294
Washington, DC 20026

Bed & Breakfast America: 1985-1986, by John Thaxton.
(Formerly: *The Great American Guest House Book.*)
Burt Franklin & Co., Inc.
235 East 44th Street
New York, NY 10017
This is part of the "Compleat Traveller" Series which also includes specific guides to B&Bs and country inns in New England, the Midwest and Rocky Mountains, the Mid-Atlantic and South, and California, Oregon and Washington State, authored by, among others, A. Hitchcock and J. Lindgren, and all published by Burt Franklin.

Christopher's Bed & Breakfast Guide to U.S. & Canada, by Bob &
   Ellen Christopher.
10 Fenway North
c/o Travel Discoveries
Milford, CT 06460

Frommer's Bed & Breakfast North America, by Hal Gieseking.
Frommer/Pasmantier Publishers
Division of Simon & Schuster
1230 Avenue of the Americas
New York, NY 10020

East Coast Bed & Breakfast Guide: New England & Mid-Atlantic, by
   Roberta Gardner.
West Coast Bed & Breakfast Guide: California—Oregon—Washington,
   by Courtia Worth and Terry Berger.
Simon & Schuster
1230 Avenue of the Americas
New York, NY 10020

The Bed & Breakfast Guide for the U.S. and Canada, by P. Featherston
   & B. Ostler.
National Bed & Breakfast Association
P.O. Box 332
Norwalk, CT 06852

Bed & Breakfast in the Northeast, by Bernice Chesler.
Guide to the Recommended Country Inns of New Jersey, Pennsylvania, Delaware, Maryland, District of Columbia, Virginia, West Virginia, by Brenda Chapin.
Guide to the Recommended Country Inns of New England, by Elizabeth Squier.
The Globe Pequot Press
Box Q, Old Chester Road
Chester, CT 06412

The New England Guest House Book, by Corinne M. Ross.
The Mid-Atlantic Guest House Book, by Corinne M. Ross.
The Southern Guest House Book by Corinne M. Ross.
East Woods Press Books
Fast & McMillan Publishers, Inc.
429 E. Boulevard
Charlotte, NC 28203

Bed & Breakfast American Style—1985, by Norman Simpson.
Berkshire Traveller Press
Stockbridge, MA 01262
1985 edition published by: Harper and Rowe.

Country Bed & Breakfast Places in Canada: A Guide to Warmth and Hospitality Along Canadian Highways and Byways, by John Thompson, also is published by the Berkshire Traveller Press.

Bed & Breakfast North America, by N.S. Buzan & L. Bodine.
Betsy Ross Publications
3057 Betsy Ross Drive
Bloomfield Hills, MI 48013

Robert R. Bensen
P.O. Box 118
Burlington, VT 05402
Publishes a list of over 200 RSOs.

Country Inns of New York State, by Robert Tolf and Roxane Rauch, and *Country Inns of New England,* by same authors.
101 Productions
834 Mission Street
San Francisco, CA 94103

Reservation Service
Organizations to List With

This Resource File lists three kinds of reservation service organizations: those with listings national in scope; those with a special focus; and, the largest group, those within each state. Use these addresses and telephone numbers to contact those organizations which appear to have the most potential for your individual needs. Use the information in Chapter 9 to help you choose. Be sure to find out which will book for you, and which publish a directory, before making your decisions.

National/International RSOs

The RSOs listed below are established ones having national or even international listings.

Bed & Breakfast Associated Reservation Services
P.O. Box 4616
Springfield, MA 01101
*215 / 885-0991

Bed & Breakfast Reservation Services International
49 Van Wyck Street
Croton-on-Hudson, NY 10520
914 / 271-6228

Bed & Breakfast Registry—North America
P.O. Box 80174
St. Paul, MN 55108
612 / 646-4238

Home Suite Homes
1470 Firebird Way
Sunnyvale, CA 94087
408 / 733-7215

The International Spareroom
P.O. Box 460
Helena, MT 59624
406 / 449-7231

The Bed & Breakfast League, Ltd.
2855 29th Street, N.W.
Washington, DC 20008
202 / 232-8718 or 800 / 368-5613

*This area code is correct.

Special-Focus RSOs

The RSOs listed below are special in the sense that they draw guests and/or hosts from a particular group, although others may be welcome. Some of these organizations have extensive listings, both national and international. We have listed here some of the more common kinds of RSO special-focus networks. The list is not exhaustive and, of course, new groups are being formed all the time. Also, check with any professional, religious or other groups to which you belong, to see if they have such a network you might join.

Educator's Vacation Alternatives
317 Piedmont Road
Santa Barbara, CA 93105
805 / 687-2947

Educators Inn
P.O. Box 603
Lynnfield, MA 01940
617 / 334-6144

Teacher's Co-Op Travel Club
P.O. Box 729
Windsor, CA 95492

Boston Bed & Breakfast
16 Ballard Street
Newton Center, MA 02159
617 / 332-4199

University Bed & Breakfast
12 Churchill Street
Brookline, MA 02146
617 / 738-1424

All of the above organizations have some connection with teaching, teaching support staff, visiting scholars, etc. Inquire if you think you might qualify as part of such a group.

B&B/Ski America & Canada
P.O. Box 5246
Incline Village, NV 89450
702 / 831-5350
For winter sports enthusiasts.

American Historic Homes
P.O. Box 336
Dana Point, CA 92629
714 / 496-7050
Lodgings in homes listed on the National Historic Register, or other landmark houses.

Commissioned Host & Toast, Inc.
P.O. Box 2177
Springfield, VA 22152
301 / 863-6525
For military personnel (including retired) wishing to lodge in or near Washington, DC.

BayHosts
1155 Bosworth Street
San Francisco, CA 04131
415 / 334-7262
A B&B agency for gays; nongays are welcome.

The League of Women Voters
Consult state office or local chapter of league.
Lodgings for league members in homes of same.

Evergreen
American Bed & Breakfast Association
P.O. Box 23294
Washington, DC 20026
703 / 237-9777

Elder Hostels
100 Boylston, Suite 200
Boston, MA 02116
Provides classes and dormitory accommodations during summer months.

The two groups above operate for those over age 50.

RCA Bed & Breakfast Publications
3975 Cascade Road, S.E.
Grand Rapids, MI 49506
This is the B&B network of the Reformed Church in America.

Homecomings
Box 1545
New Milford, CT 06776
Lodgings with and for Unitarians, Quakers, Ethical Culturists, Humanists, etc.

SERVAS
U.S. Servas Committee
11 John Street, Room 406
New York, NY 10038
212 / 267-0252
A non-profit, interfaith, interracial group.

State by State RSOs

These RSOs, for almost all states and the District of Columbia, are listed alphabetically by city within each state. Some cover the whole state, or even several states, overlapping nearby boundaries. Some have listings around the country as well. Some network with other RSOs to provide fairly intense national coverage. If there is no RSO listed for your state try a national RSO for suggestions. Or, look in a guidebook and get in touch with some other B&Bs in your state to find out what RSOs they are using.

Alabama

Bed & Breakfast Birmingham
P.O. Box 31328
Birmingham, AL 35222
205 / 591-6406

Bed & Breakfast Mobile
P.O. Box 66261
Mobile, AL 36606
205 / 473-2939

Brunton's Bed & Breakfast
P.O. Box 1006
Scottsboro, AL 35768
205 / 259-1298

Alaska

Anchorage B&B/Alaska Private
    Lodgings
P.O. Box 110135 South Station
Anchorage, AK 99511
907 / 345-2222

Stay With a Friend
Box 173, 3605 Arctic Blvd.
Anchorage, AK 99503
907 / 274-6445 (9 a.m.-5.p.m.)

Fairbanks Bread & Breakfast
Box 74573
Fairbanks, AK 99707
907 / 452-4957

Alaska Bed & Breakfast Assn.
526 Seward Street
Juneau, AK 99801
907 / 586-2959

Dawson's Bed & Breakfast
1941 Glacier Highway
Juneau, AK 99801
907 / 586-9708

Ketchikan Bed & Breakfast
Box 7735
Ketchikan, AK 99901
907 / 225-3860 or 225-9277

Kodiak Bed & Breakfast
P.O. Box 1221
Kodiak, AK 99615
907 / 486-4522 or 486-5200

Arizona

Bed & Breakfast in Arizona
8433 N. Black Canyon Hwy.,
Suite 160
Phoenix, AZ 85021
602 / 995-2831

Accommodations in Arizona / Mi
    Casa-Su Casa Bed & Breakfast
P.O. Box 950
Tempe, AZ 85281
602 / 990-0682

157

Bed & Breakfast Scottsdale
P.O. Box 624
Scottsdale, AZ 85252
602 / 998-7044

Scottsdale/San Diego B&B
P.O. Box 995
Scottsdale, AZ 85258
602 / 998-7044

Barbara's Bed & Breakfast
P.O. Box 13603
Tucson, AZ 85732
602 / 886-5847

Arkansas

Ozark B&B
1567 Porter
Bakersville, AR 72501
501 / 793-4289

California

Visitors Advisory Service
1516 Oak Street, No. 327
Alameda, CA 94501
415 / 521-9366

Eye Openers Bed & Breakfast
P.O. Box 694
Altadena, CA 91001
818 / 684-4428

Big Yellow Sunflower B&B
235 Sky Oaks Drive
Angwin, CA 94508
707 / 965-3885 or 965-7627

Digs West
8191 Crowley Circle
Buena Park, CA 90621
714 / 739-1669

Homestay
P.O. Box 326
Cambria, CA 93428
805 / 927-4613

Bed & Breakfast West Coast
4744 Third Street
Carpinteria, CA 93013
805 / 684-3523

California B&B Inn Service
P.O. Box 1256
Chico, CA 95927
916 / 343-9733

B&B of San Diego
P.O. Box 1006
Coronado, CA 93103
602 / 952-9383

B&B of Southern California
P.O. Box 218
Fullerton, CA 92632
714 / 738-8361

Rent A Room
11531 Varna Street
Garden Grove, CA 92640
714 / 638-1406

Bed & Breakfast International
151 Ardmore Road
Kensington, CA 94707
415 / 527-8836

Bed & Breakfast Hospitality
823 La Mirada Avenue
Leucadia, CA 92024
619 / 436-6850

Houseguests, Inc.
672 South Lafayette Park Place,
    No. 42
Los Angeles, CA 90057
213 / 388-0491

Megan's Friends
1296 Galleon Way, No. 2
Los Osos, CA 93401
805 / 544-4406

Napa Valley B&B Referral
1834 First Street
Napa, CA 94559
707 / 224-4667

Bed & Breakfast/Monterey
  Peninsula
P.O. Box 1193
Pebble Beach, CA 93953
408 / 372-7425

Briggs House / Sacramento
  Innkeepers Association
2209 Capitol Avenue
Sacramento, CA 95816
916 / 441-3214

California Bed'n Breakfast
P.O. Box 1551
Sacramento, CA 95807
Phone not applicable/by mail only

Bed and Breakfast Almanac
Box 295
St. Helena, CA 94574
707 / 963-0852

Bed & Breakfast Exchange
P.O. Box 88
St. Helena, CA 94574
707 / 963-7756

Carolyn's Bed & Breakfast Homes
P.O. Box 84776
San Diego, CA 92138
619 / 435-5009

American Family Inn/Bed &
  Breakfast San Francisco
Box 349
San Francisco, CA 94101
415 / 931-3083

University Bed & Breakfast
1387 Sixth Avenue
San Francisco, CA 94122
415 / 661-8940

Christian Bed & Breakfast
Box 388
San Juan Capistrano, CA 92693
714 / 496-7050

Hospitality Plus
Box 388
San Juan Capistrano, CA 92693
714 / 496-7050

Wine Country Bed & Breakfast
P.O. Box 3211
Santa Rosa, CA 95403
707 / 539-1183

California Houseguests
  International
18533 Burbank Blvd., No. 190
Tarzana, CA 91356
818 / 344-7878

Mona's Bed & Breakfast Homes
P.O. Box 1805
Temecula, CA 92390
714 / 676-4729

Bed & Breakfast Approved Hosts
10890 Galvin
Ventura, CA 93004
805 / 647-0651

Bed & Breakfast of Los Angeles
32127 Harborview Lane/
    or 32074 Waterside
Westlake Village, CA 91361
818 / 889-7325 or 889-8870

CoHost America's Bed &
  Breakfast
P.O. Box 9302
Whittier, CA 90608
213 / 699-8427

Colorado

B&B of Boulder, Inc.
Box 6061
Boulder, CO 80302
303 / 442-6664

Bed & Breakfast Rocky
    Mountains
P.O. Box 804
Colorado Springs, CO 80901
303 / 630-3433

Bed & Breakfast Colorado
P.O. Box 20596
Denver, CO 80220
303 / 333-3340

Bed & Breakfast Durango
862 Main St., Suite 222
Durango, CO 81301
303 / 247-2223

Vail Bed & Breakfast
P.O. Box 491
Vail, CO 81658
303 / 476-1225

Connecticut

Nautilus Bed & Breakfast
133 Phoenix Drive
Groton, CT 06340
203 / 448-1538

B&B Ltd. in New Haven
P.O. Box 216
New Haven, CT 06513
203 / 469-3260

Seacoast Landings
21 Fuller Street
New London, CT 06320
203 / 442-1940

Covered Bridge Bed & Breakfast
West Cornwall, CT 06796
203 / 672-6052

Nutmeg Bed & Breakfast
56 Fox Chase Lane
West Hartford, CT 06107
203 / 236-6698

Delaware

Bed & Breakfast of Delaware
1804 Breen Lane
Wilmington, DE 19810
302 / 475-0340

District of Columbia

Bed & Breakfast Ltd. of
    Washington, D.C.
P.O. Box 12011
Washington, DC 20005
202 / 328-3510

Sweet Dreams and Toast, Inc.
P.O. Box 4835-0035
Washington, DC 20008
202 / 483-9191

Florida

B&B Registry of Florida
Box 322
Jupiter, FL 33458
305 / 746-2545

Tropical Isles B&B Co.
P.O. Box 490382
Key Biscayne, FL 33149
305 / 361-2937

Suncoast Accommodations
P.O. Box 8334
Madeira Beach, FL 33708
813 / 393-7020

B&B of the Florida Keys and East
    Coast
5 Man-O-War Drive,
    P.O. Box 1373
Marathon, FL 33050
305 / 743-4118 or 201 / 223-5979
    (August 1 to October 15)

Florida & England Bed &
    Breakfast Accommodations
P.O. Box 12
Palm Harbor, FL 33563
813 / 784-5118

B&B Suncoast Accommodations
8690 Gulf Blvd.
St. Petersburg Beach, FL 33706
813 / 360-1753

Bed & Breakfast Company
P.O Box 262
South Miami, FL 33243
305 / 661-3270

Tallahassee Bed & Breakfast
3023 Windy Hill Lane
Tallahassee, FL 32308
904 / 385-3768 or 421-5220

AAA Bed & Breakfast of
    Florida, Inc.
P.O. Box 1316
Winter Park, FL 32790
305 / 628-3233

Georgia

Atlanta Hospitality
2472 Lauderdale Drive, N.E.
Atlanta, GA 30345
404 / 493-1930

Bed & Breakfast Atlanta
1221 Fairview Road, N.E.
Atlanta, GA 30306
404 / 378-6026

Bed & Breakfast Hideaway
    Homes
Dial Star Route Box 76
Blue Ridge, GA 30513
404 / 632-2411 or 632-3669

Bed & Breakfast-Savannah
117 Gordon Street West at
Chatham Square
Savannah, GA 31401
912 / 238-0518 or 233-9481

Intimate Inns of Savannah
19 W. Perry Street
Savannah, GA 31401
912 / 233-6890

Savannah Historic Inns and
    Guest Houses
1900 Lincoln Street
Savannah, GA 31401
912 / BED-ROOM (233-7666)

Quail Country Bed & Breakfast
1104 Old Monticello Road
Thomasville, GA 31792
912 / 226-7218 or 226-6882

Hawaii

Go Native . . . . Hawaii
130 Puhili Street
Hilo, HI 96720
808 / 961-2080

Pacific-Hawaii B&B
19 Kai Nani Place
Kailua, Oahu, HI 96734
808 / 262-6026 or 254-5115

Bed & Breakfast Hawaii
P.O. Box 449
Kapaa, HI 96746
808 / 822-7771

Idaho

Phoenix Bed & Breakfast
117 So. Second Avenue
Sandpoint, ID 83864
208 / 263-4018

Illinois

Bed & Breakfast of Chicago
P.O. Box 14088
Chicago, IL 60614
312 / 951-0085

Bed & Board/America Inc.
7308 W. Madison Avenue
Forest Park, IL 60130
312 / 771-8100

Bed & Breakfast Quad Cities
2530—29½ Street
Rock Island, IL 61201
309 / 788-9233

Indiana

Tammy Galm B&B
P.O. Box 546
Nashville, IN 47448

Iowa

Bed & Breakfast in Iowa, Ltd.
7104 Franklin Avenue
Des Moines, IA 50322
515 / 277-9018

Kansas

Kansas City Bed & Breakfast
P.O. Box 14781
Lenexa, KS 66215
913 / 268-4214

Kansas City B&B
15416 Johnson Drive
Shawnee, KS 66217

Kentucky

Kentucky Homes Bed & Breakfast
1431 St. James Court
Louisville, KY 40208
502 / 635-7341 or 452-6629

Louisiana

Louisiana Hospitality
    Services, Inc.
P.O. Box 80717
Baton Rouge, LA 70898
504 / 769-0366

Southern Comfort B&B
2856 Hundred Oaks
Baton Rouge, LA 70808
504 / 346-1928

Bed & Breakfast Inc.
1236 Decatur Street
New Orleans, LA 70116
504 / 525-4640

Bed & Breakfast of
    Louisiana and Tours
P.O. Box 8128
New Orleans, LA 70182
504 / 949-6705 or 949-4570

New Orleans Bed & Breakfast
P.O. Box 8163
New Orleans, LA 70182
504 / 949-6705 or 949-4570

Maine

B&B Down East, Ltd.
Box 547, Macomber Mill Road
Eastbrook, ME 04634
207 / 565-3517

B&B Registry of Maine
32 Colonial Village
Falmouth, ME 04105
207 / 781-4528

B&B Accommodations
P.O. Box 805
Rockland, ME 08401
207 / 594-8275

Maryland

The Maryland Registry
℅ Sharp-Adams
33 West Street
Annapolis, MD 21401
301 / 269-6232 or 261-2233

Massachusetts

Bed & Breakfast Associates Bay
    Colony, Ltd.
P.O. Box 166,
    Babson Park Branch
Boston, MA 02157
617 / 872-6990

B&B Brookline/Boston
Box 732
Brookline, MA 02146
617 / 369-8416

Greater Boston Hospitality
P.O. Box 1142
Brookline, MA 02146
617 / 734-0807

Bed & Breakfast à la Cambridge
    & Greater Boston
73 Kirkland Street
Cambridge, MA 02138
617 / 576-1492

House Guests, Cape Cod
Box 8AR
Dennis, MA 02638
617 / 398-0787

B&B in Minuteman Country
8 Linmoor Terrace
Lexington, MA 02173
617 / 861-7063

Pineapple Hospitality, Inc.
384 Rodney French Blvd.
New Bedford, MA 02744
617 / 990-1696

Host Homes of Boston
P.O. Box 117
Newton, MA 02168
617 / 244-1308

New England Bed & Breakfast
1045 Centre Street
Newton, MA 02159
617 / 244-2112 or 498-9810

Be Our Guest B&B
P.O.Box 1333
Plymouth, MA 02360
617 / 746-1208

Pioneer Valley Bed & Breakfast
141 Newton Road
Springfield, MA 01108
413 / 268-7244

Sturbridge Bed & Breakfast
141 Newton Road
Springfield, MA 01118
413 / 268-7244

Bed & Breakfast Cape Cod
Box 341
West Hyannisport, MA 02672
617 / 775-2772

Berkshire Bed & Breakfast of
    Western Massachusetts
43 Main Street
Williamsburg, MA 01096-0211
413 / 268-7244

Hampshire Hills Bed &
    Breakfast Assn.
P.O. Box 307
Williamsburg, MA 01096
413 / 634-5529

Michigan

Betsy Ross Bed & Breakfast
3067 Betsy Ross Drive
Bloomfield Hills, MI 48013
313 / 647-1158 or 646-5357

B&B of Grand Rapids
344 College Avenue, S.E.
Grand Rapids, MI 49503
616 / 451-4849 or 456-7121

Hometels of Michigan
8019 Hendrie Street
Huntington Woods, MI 48070

Minnesota

Bed & Breakfast Upper Midwest
P.O. Box 28036
Crystal Lake, MN 55428
612 / 535-7135

Uptown-Lake District B&B
2000 Aldrich Avenue S.
Minneapolis, MN 55405
612 / 872-7884

Mississippi

Lincoln Ltd. Bed & Breakfast
Box 3479
Meridian, MS 39301
601 / 482-5483

Natchez Pilgrimage Tours
P.O. Box 347
Natchez, MS 39120
800 / 647-6742 or 601 / 446-6631

Missouri

Ozark Mountain Country B&B
Box 295
Branson, MO 65616
417 / 334-5077 or 334-4270

Truman Country Bed & Breakfast
424 N. Pleasant
Independence, MO 64050
816 / 254-6657

Lexington Bed & Breakfast
115 N. 18th Street
Lexington, MO 64607
816 / 259-4163

Midwest Host Bed & Breakfast
P.O. Box 27
Saginaw, MO 64846
417 / 782-9112

Bed & Breakfast St. Louis
16 Green Acres
St. Louis, MO 63137
314 / 868-2335

River Country Bed & Breakfast
1 Grandview Heights
St. Louis, MO 63131
417 / 965-4328

Montana

Western Bed & Breakfast Hosts
P.O. Box 322
Kalispell, MT 59901
406 / 257-4476

Nebraska

B&B of Nebraska
1426 28th Avenue
Columbus, NE 68601
402 / 564-7591

New Hampshire

New Hampshire B&B
RFD 3, Box 53
Laconia, NH 03246
603 / 279-8348

New Jersey

Town and Country Bed &
    Breakfast
P.O. Box 301
Lambertville, NJ 08530
609 / 397-8399

B&B of New Jersey
103 Godwin Avenue, Suite 132
Midland Park, NJ 07432
201 / 444-7409

New Mexico

Bed & Breakfast Sunbelt
1310 Calle de Ranchero, N.E.
Albuquerque, NM 87106
501 / 265-7071

Bed & Breakfast of Santa Fe
218 E. Buena Vista Street
Santa Fe, NM 87501
505 / 982-3332

New York

Travelers Retreat
RD 3, Melvin Lane
Baldwinsville, NY 13027
315 / 638-8664 (Syracuse) or
    518 / 489-8211 (Albany)

Bed & Breakfast USA, Ltd.
P.O. Box 606
Croton-on-Hudson, NY 10521
914 / 271-6228

Alternative Lodgings, Inc.
P.O. Box 1782
East Hampton, NY 11937
516 / 324-9449

Hampton Hosts
P.O. Box 507
East Hampton, NY 11937
516 / 324-9351 or 212 / 696-1938

Lodgings Plus Bed & Breakfast
P.O. Box 279
East Hampton, NY 11937
212 / 858-9589 or 516 / 324-6740

Hampton Bed & Breakfast
  Registry
Box 695
East Moriches, NY 11940
516 / 367-4707

Bed & Breakfast Rochester
P.O. Box 444
Fairport, NY 14450
716 / 223-8510 or 223-8877

Bed & Breakfast Leatherstocking/
  Central N.Y.
389 Brockway Road
Frankfort, NY 13340
315 / 733-0040

Cherry Valley Ventures
6119 Cherry Valley Turnpike
Lafayette, NY 13084
315 / 677-9723

North Country B&B
  Reservation Service
Box 286, The Barn
Lake Placid, NY 12946
518 / 523-3739

B&B Group
  (New Yorkers at Home)
301 E. 60th St.
New York, NY 10022
212 / 838-7015

Urban Ventures/B&B in the
  Big Apple
P.O. Box 426
New York, NY 10024
212 / 594-5650

Rainbow Hospitality B&B
9348 Hennepin Avenue
Niagara Falls, NY 14304
716 / 283-4794 or 754-8877 or
  283-1400

A Reasonable Alternative
117 Spring Street
Port Jefferson, NY 17777
516 / 928-4034

Bed & Breakfast of Central
  New York
1846 Bellevue Avenue
Syracuse, NY 13204
315 / 472-5050

East End Bed & Breakfast, Inc.
P.O. Box 178
West Hampton, NY 11977
516 / 288-4488

North Carolina

Charlotte B&B—The Chimneys
1700-2 DeLane Avenue
Charlotte, NC 28211
704 / 366-0979

Bed & Breakfast/Greensboro
210 W. Bessemer Ave.
Greensboro, NC 27401
919 / 272-6248

Ohio

Chillicothe Bed & Breakfast
189 North High St.
Chillicothe, OH 45601
614 / 773-3636

Private Lodgings, Inc.
P.O. Box 18590
Cleveland, OH 44118
216 / 321-3213

Columbus Bed & Breakfast
769 S. Third Street
Columbus, OH 43206
614 / 444-8888 or 443-3680

Buckeye Bed & Breakfast
P.O. Box 130
Powell, OH 43065
614 / 548-4555

Oregon

Bend Bed & Breakfast
19838 Ponderosa Drive
Bend, OR 97701
503 / 388-3007

Galluci Hosts, Hostels, B&B
P.O. Box 1303
Lake Oswego, OR 97034
503 / 636-6933

Bed & Breakfast Oregon
5733 S.W. Dickinson St.
Portland, OR 97219
503 / 245-0642

Northwest Bed & Breakfast
7707 S.W. Locust Street
Portland, OR 97223
503 / 246-8366

Pennsylvania

B&B of Southeast Pennsylvania
Box 278, RD 1
Barto, PA 19504
215 / 845-3526

Bed & Breakfast Pocono
   Northeast
P.O. Box 115
Bear Creek, PA 18602
717 / 472-3145

Bed & Breakfast of Philadelphia
P.O. Box 680
Devon, PA 19333
215 / 688-1633

Bed & Breakfast of Lancaster
   County
P.O. Box 215
Elm, PA 17521
717 / 627-1890

Bed & Breakfast of
   Chester County
P.O. Box 825
Kennett Square, PA 19348
215 / 444-1367

Nissly's Olde Home Inns
   & Guest Apts.
624 West Chestnut St.
Lancaster, PA 17602
717 / 392-2311 or 866-4926

B&B of Philadelphia
P.O. Box 101
Oreland, PA 19075
215 / 884-1084

Bed & Breakfast/Center City
1908 Spruce Street
Philadelphia, PA 19103
215 / 735-1137

Rest & Repast B&B Service
P.O. Box 126
Pine Grove Mills, PA 16868
814 / 238-1484

Pittsburgh Bed & Breakfast
P.O. Box 25353
Pittsburgh, PA 15242
412 / 241-5746

Endless Mountains
   Reservation Service
Box 294B
Union Dale, PA 18470
717 / 679-2425

Country Cousins B&B
228 W. Main Street
Waynesboro, PA 17268
717 / 762-2722

Rhode Island

Bed & Breakfast Registry
Castle Keep, 44 Everett
Newport, RI 02840
401 / 846-0362

Guest House Association
23 Brinley Street
Newport, RI 02840
401 / 849-7645

At Home in New England
P.O. Box 25
Saunderstown, RI 02874
401 / 294-3808

South Carolina

Bay Street Accommodations
601 Bay Street
Beaufort, SC 29902
803 / 524-7720

Charleston Society B&B
84 Murray Blvd.
Charleston, SC 29401
803 / 723-4948

Historic Charleston B&B
43 Legare Street
Charleston, SC 29401
803 / 722-6606

Charleston East Bed & Breakfast
1031 Tall Pine Road
Mount Pleasant, SC 29464
803 / 884-8208

South Dakota

Bed & Breakfast of South Dakota
P.O. Box 80137
Sioux Falls, SD 57116
605 / 528-6571 or 339-0759

Tennessee

Grinders Switch B&B
   Reservation Agency
Route 2, Box 44
Centerville, TN 37033
615 / 729-5002

Hospitality at Home, Inc.
Rt. 1, Buttermilk Road
Lenoir City, TN 37771
615 / 693-3500

Bed & Breakfast in Memphis
P.O. Box 41621
Memphis, TN 38104
901 / 726-5920

River Rendezvous
P.O. Box 240001
Memphis, TN 38124
901 / 767-5296

Nashville Bed & Breakfast
P.O. Box 15651
Nashville, TN 37215
615 / 298-5674

Host Homes of Tennessee
   (A B&B Group)
P.O. Box 110227
Nashville, TN 37222
615 / 331-5244

Texas

B&B Society of Houston
4432 Holt
Bellaire, TX 77401
713 / 666-6372

Sand Dollar Hospitality
3605 Mendenhall
Corpus Christi, TX 78415
512 / 853-1222

Bed & Breakfast Texas Style
4224 W. Red Bird Lane
Dallas, TX 75237
214 / 298-8586

Bed & Breakfast Society
  International
307 W. Main Street
Fredericksburg, TX 78624
512 / 997-4712

Bed & Breakfast in
  Fredericksburg
307 West Main Street
Fredericksburg, TX 78624
512 / 997-4712

Bed & Breakfast of Dallas/
  Ft. Worth
1701 W. Greenville Avenue,
  No. 304
Richardson, TX 77401

Bed & Breakfast Hosts of
  San Antonio
166 Rockhill
San Antonio, TX 78209
512 / 824-8036

Utah

Bed & Breakfast Association
  of Utah
P.O. Box 16465
Salt Lake City, UT 84116
801 / 532-7076

Vermont

American B&B in New England
Box 983
St. Albans, VT 05478
802 / 524-4731

Vermont Bed & Breakfast
Box 139, Brown's Trace
Jericho, VT 05465
802 / 899-2354

Virginia

Princely/Bed & Breakfast, Ltd.
819 Prince Street
Alexandria, VA 22314
703 / 683-2159

Blue Ridge B&B
Rte. 1, Box 517
Bluemont, VA 22012
703 / 955-3955

Guest Houses B&B, Inc.
P.O. Box 5737
Charlottesville, VA 22905
804 / 979-7264 (12-5 P.M.)

Sojourners Bed & Breakfast
3609 Tanglewood Lane
Lynchburg, VA 24503
804 / 384-1655

Bed and Breakfast of
  Tidewater Virginia
P.O. Box 3343
Norfolk, VA 23514
804 / 627-1983 or 627-9409

Bensonhouse of Richmond
P.O. Box 15131
Richmond, VA 23227
804 / 648-7560 or 321-6277

The Travel Tree
P.O. Box 838
Williamsburg, VA 23187
804 / 229-4037 or 565-2236

Washington

B&B Service (BABS)
P.O. Box 5025
Bellingham, WA 98227
203 / 733-8642

RSVP Bed & Breakfast
  Reservation Service
P.O. Box 778
Ferndale, WA 98248
206 / 384-6586

Guest House Bed & Breakfast
835 E. Christenson Road
Greenback, WA 98253
206 / 678-3115

Whidbey Island B&B Assn.
P.O. Box 259
Langley, WA 98260
206 / 678-3115

Traveller's Bed & Breakfast
P.O. Box 492
Mercer Island, WA 98040
206 / 232-2345

Pacific Bed & Breakfast
701 N.W. 60th Street
Seattle, WA 98107
206 / 784-0539

West Coast Bed & Breakfast Club
11304 20th Place, S.W.
Seattle, WA 98146
206 / 246-2650

INNterlodging Bed & Breakfast
P.O. Box 7044
Tacoma, WA 98407
206 / 756-0343

Wisconsin

Bed & Breakfast in Door Country
Route 2
Algoma, WI 54201
414 / 743-9742

Bed & Breakfast of Milwaukee
3017 N. Downer Avenue
Milwaukee, WI 53211
414 / 342-5030

Inn-Starting Information

This Resource File lists the names and addresses of several businesses devoted to helping beginners find, purchase and operate a country inn. This list is not extensive and is intended only to help you get started. Contact any innkeepers near you, as well. Many innkeepers now offer seminars on buying and running country inns. There may be one or more in your area. We also list one book on the subject.

INNovations
108 Loudoun Street, S.W.
Craig & Amy DeRemer
Leesburg, VA 22075
703 / 777-1806

Deborah Sakach
3326 Mesa Vista
Dana Point, CA 92629
714 / 496-6953

William Oates and Associates
36 High Street
Brattleboro, VT 05301
802 / 254-5931

How to Open a Country Inn
by Karen L. Etsell & Elaine C. Brennan
The Berkshire Traveller Press
Stockbridge, MA 01262

Historic Preservation Officers

This Resource File lists the title, address and telephone number of the preservation officer in each state of the United States. These are the places to contact about historic preservation procedures, rehabilitation procedures and the tax credits associated with them.

Alabama

Executive Director
Alabama Historical Commission
725 Monroe Street
Montgomery, AL 36130
205 / 261-3184

Alaska

Chief of History and Archeology, Division of Parks
Department of Natural Resources
225A Cordova Street
Anchorage, AK 99501
907 / 274-4676

Arizona

Chief, Office of Historic Preservation
Arizona State Parks
1688 West Adams
Phoenix, AZ 85007
602 / 255-4174

Arkansas

Director, Arkansas Historic Preservation Program
The Heritage Center, Suite 200
225 East Markham
Little Rock, AR 72201
501 / 371-2763

California

State Historic Preservation Officer
Office of Historic Preservation
Department of Parks and Recreation
P.O. Box 2390
Sacramento, CA 95811
916 / 445-8006

Colorado

State Historic Preservation Officer
Colorado Heritage Center
1300 Broadway
Denver, CO 80203
303 / 886-2136

Connecticut

Director, Connecticut Historical Commission
59 South Prospect Street
Hartford, CT 06106
203 / 566-3005

Delaware

Director, Division of Historical and Cultural Affairs
Hall of Records
Dover, DE 19901
302 / 736-5314

District of Columbia

Director, Department of Consumer and Regulatory Affairs
614 H Street, N.W.
Washington, DC 20001
202 / 727-7360

Florida

Director, Division of Archives, History, and Records Management
Department of State
The Capitol
Tallahassee, FL 32301
904 / 487-2333

Georgia

Chief, Historic Preservation Section
Department of Natural Resources
270 Washington Street, S.W., Room 703C
Atlanta, GA 30334
404 / 656-2840

Hawaii

State Historic Preservation Officer
Department of Land and Natural Resources
P.O. Box 621
Honolulu, HI 96809
808 / 548-7460

Idaho

Historic Preservation Coordinator
Idaho Historical Society
610 North Julia Davis Drive
Boise, ID 83706
208 / 334-2120

Illinois

Director, Department of Conservation
State Office Building
400 South Spring Street
Springfield, IL 62706
217 / 782-6302

Indiana

Director, Department of Natural Resources
608 State Office Building
Indianapolis, IN 46204
317 / 232-4020

Iowa

Director, Iowa State Historical Department
Office of Historic Preservation, Historical Building
East 12th Street and Grand Avenue
Des Moines, IA 50319
515 / 281-5113

Kansas

Executive Director, Kansas State Historical Society
120 West 10th Street
Topeka, KS 66612
913 / 296-3251

Kentucky

State Historical Preservation Officer
Director, Kentucky Heritage Council
Capital Plaza Tower, 12th Floor
Frankfort, KY 40601
502 / 564-7005

Louisiana

Assistant Secretary, Office of Cultural Development
P.O. Box 44247
Baton Rouge, LA 70804
504 / 925-3884

Maine

Director, Maine Preservation Commission
55 Capitol, Station 65
Augusta, ME 04333
207 / 289-2133

Maryland

State Historic Preservation Officer
John Shaw House
21 State Circle
Annapolis, MD 21401
301 / 269-2851

Massachusetts

Executive Director, Massachusetts Historical Commission
294 Washington Street
Boston, MA 02108
617 / 727-8470

Michigan

Director, History Division
Department of State
208 North Capitol
Lansing, MI 48918
517 / 373-6362

Minnesota

Director, Minnesota Historical Society
690 Cedar Street
St. Paul, MN 55101
612 / 296-2747

Mississippi

Director
State of Mississippi
Department of Archives and History
P.O. Box 571
Jackson, MS 39205
601 / 359-1424

Missouri

Director
State Department of Natural Resources
P.O. Box 176
Jefferson City, MO 65102
314 / 751-4422

Montana

State Historic Preservation Officer
Montana Historical Society
225 North Roberts Street
Veterans Memorial Building
Helena, MT 59620
406 / 444-2694

Nebraska

Director
Nebraska State Historical Society
1500 R Street, P.O. Box 82554
Lincoln, NB 68508
402 / 471-3850

Nevada

Director
Department of Conservation and Natural Resources
Nye Building, Room 213
201 South Fall Street
Carson City, NV 89710
702 / 885-4360

New Hampshire

Commissioner
Department of Resources and Economic Development
P.O. Box 856
Concord, NH 03301
603 / 271-2411

New Jersey

Commissioner
Department of Environmental Protection
CN 402
Trenton, NJ 08625
609 / 292-2885

New Mexico

State Historic Preservation Officer
Historic Preservation Division
Office of Cultural Affairs
Villa Rivera, Room 101
228 East Palace Avenue
Santa Fe, NM 87503
505 / 827-8320

New York

Commissioner
Office of Parks, Recreation, and Historic Preservation
Agency Building #1, Empire State Plaza
Albany, NY 12238
518 / 474-0697

North Carolina

Director, Division of Archives and History
Department of Cultural Resources
109 East Jones Street
Raleigh, NC 27611
919 / 733-7305

North Dakota

Superintendent
State Historical Society of North Dakota
Liberty Memorial Building
Bismarck, ND 58501
701 / 224-2667

Ohio

State Historic Preservation Officer
Ohio Historical Society
Interstate 71 at 17th Avenue
Columbus, OH 43211
614 / 466-1500

Oklahoma

State Historic Preservation Officer
Oklahoma Historical Society
Historical Building
2100 North Lincoln
Oklahoma City, OK 73105
405 / 521-2491

Oregon

State Parks Superintendent
525 Trade Street, SE
Salem, OR 97310
503 / 378-5019

Pennsylvania

State Historic Preservation Officer
Pennsylvania Historical and Museum Commission
P.O. Box 1026
Harrisburg, PA 17108
717 / 787-2891

Rhode Island

Director
Rhode Island Department of Community Affairs
150 Washington Street
Providence, RI 02903
401 / 277-2850

South Carolina

Director
Department of Archives and History
1430 Senate Street
Columbia, SC 29211
803 / 758-5816

South Dakota

State Historic Preservation Officer
Historical Preservation Center
University of South Dakota, Alumni House
Vermillion, SD 57069
605 / 773-3458

Tennessee

State Historic Preservation Officer
Department of Conservation
701 Broadway
Nashville, TN 37219
615 / 741-2301

Texas

Executive Director
Texas State Historical Commission
P.O. Box 12276
Capitol Station
Austin, TX 78711
512 / 475-3092

Utah

State Historic Preservation Officer
Utah State Historical Society
300 Rio Grande
Salt Lake City, UT 84101
801 / 533-7039

Vermont

Secretary
Agency of Development and Community Affairs
Pavilion Office Building
Montpelier, VT 05602
802 / 828-3211

Virginia

Executive Director
Virginia Historic Landmarks Commission
221 Governor Street
Richmond, VA 23219
804 / 786-3143

Washington

State Historic Preservation Officer
111 West 21st Avenue, KL-11
Olympia, WA 98504
206 / 753-4011

West Virginia

Commissioner
Department of Culture and History
State Capitol Complex
Charleston, WV 25304
304 / 348-0244

Wisconsin

Director, Historic Preservation Division
State Historical Society of Wisconsin
816 State Street
Madison, WI 53706
608 / 262-3266

Wyoming

Director
Wyoming Recreation Commission
1920 Thomes Street
Cheyenne, WY 82002
307 / 777-7695

State Tourism Offices

U se these addresses to contact your tourism office for information about B&B regulations in your state. If they have listings of tourist accommodations which they circulate, ask to be included. They might also provide free vacation/travel brochures for you to give your guests.

Alabama

Alabama Bureau of Publicity and Information
532 South Perry Street
Montgomery, AL 36104
205 / 832-5510
800 / 392-8096 (within Alabama)
800 / 252-2262 (from outside Alabama)

Alaska

Alaska Division of Tourism
Department of Commerce & Economic Development
Pouch E-445
Juneau, AK 99801
907 / 465-2010

Arizona

Arizona Office of Tourism
3507 North Central Avenue, Suite 506
Phoenix, AZ 85012
602 / 255-3618

Arkansas

Arkansas Department of Parks and Tourism
1 Capitol Mall
Little Rock, AR 72201
501 / 371-7777
800 / 482-8999 (within Arkansas)

California

California Office of Tourism
Commerce Department
1121 L Street
Sacramento, CA 95814
916 / 322-1396

Colorado

Colorado Office of Tourism
5500 So. Syracuse Circle, Suite 267
Englewood, CO 80111
303 / 779-1067

Connecticut

Connecticut Department of Economic Development
Tourism Information
210 Washington Street
Hartford, CT 06106
203 / 566-3948
800 / 842-7492 (within Connecticut)

Delaware

Delaware State Travel Service
P.O. Box 1401, 99 Kings Highway
Dover, DE 19903
302 / 736-4271
800 / 282-8667 (within Delaware)
800 / 441-8846 (from outside Delaware)

District of Columbia

Washington, D.C. Convention and Visitors Association
1575 I Street, N.W., Suite 250
Washington, DC 20005
202 / 789-7000

Florida

Florida Division of Tourism
126 Van Buren Street
Tallahassee, FL 32301
904 / 487-1462

Georgia

Georgia Department of Industry and Trade
Tourist Division
Box 1776
Atlanta, GA 30301
404 / 656-3590

Hawaii

Hawaii Visitors Bureau
2270 Kalakaua Avenue, Suite 801
Honolulu, HI 96815
808 / 923-1811

Idaho

Idaho Division of Tourism and Industrial Development
Capitol Building, Room 108
Boise, ID 83720
208 / 334-2470
800 / 635-7820 (from outside Idaho)

Illinois

Illinois Office of Tourism
620 East Adams Street
Springfield, IL 62706
217 / 782-7139
800 / 252-8987 (within Illinois)
800 / 637-8560 (from neighboring states)

Indiana

Indiana Department of Commerce
Tourism Division
1 North Capitol Ave., Suite 700
Indianapolis, IN 46204
317 / 232-8860
800 / 662-4464 (within Indiana)
800 / 858-8073 (from neighboring states)

Iowa

Iowa Development Commission
Tourist Development Division
600 East Court Avenue, Suite A
Des Moines, IA 50309
515 / 281-3251

Kansas

Kansas State Department of Travel & Tourism
503 Kansas Avenue, 6th Floor
Topeka, KN 66603
913 / 296-2009

Kentucky

Kentucky Travel
Capitol Plaza
Frankfort, KY 40601
502 / 564-4930
800 / 372-2961 (within Kentucky)

Louisiana

Louisiana Office of Tourism
Inquiry Department
P.O. Box 94291
Baton Rouge, LA 70804
504 / 925-3860
800 / 231-4730 (from outside Louisiana)

Maine

Maine Publicity Bureau
97 Winthrop Street
Hallowell, ME 04347
207 / 289-2423

Maryland

Maryland State Government Tourist Information
1748 Forest Drive
Annapolis, MD 21401
301 / 269-3517

Massachusetts

Massachusetts Tourism Department
Department of Commerce and Development
100 Cambridge Street, 13th Floor
Boston, MA 02202
617 / 727-3201
800 / 632-8038 (within Massachusetts)

Michigan

Travel Bureau
Michigan Department of Commerce
P.O. Box 30226
Lansing, MI 48909
517 / 373-1195
800 / 292-2520 (within Michigan)
800 / 248-5700 (from outside Michigan)

Minnesota

Minnesota Tourist Information Center
240 Bremer Building, 41 North Robert St.
St. Paul, MN 55101
612 / 296-5029
800 / 652-9747 (within Minnesota)
800 / 328-1461 (from outside Minnesota)

Mississippi

Mississippi Division of Tourism
P.O. Box 849
Jackson, MS 39205
601 / 359-3414
800 / 962-2346 (within Mississippi)

Missouri

Missouri Division of Tourism
P.O. Box 1055
Jefferson City, MO 65102
314 / 751-4133

Montana

Montana Department of Commerce
Travel Promotion Division
1424 9th Avenue
Helena, MT 59620
406 / 444-2654
800 / 548-3390 (from outside Montana)

Nebraska

Nebraska Division of Travel and Tourism
P.O. Box 94666
Lincoln, NB 68509
402 / 471-3796
800 / 742-7595 (within Nebraska)
800 / 228-4307 (from outside Nebraska)

Nevada

Nevada Commission of Tourism
Capitol Complex
600 East Williams Street
Carson City, NV 89710
702 / 885-4322

New Hampshire

New Hampshire Division of Economic Development
Office of Vacation Information
P.O. Box 856
Concord, NH 03301
603 / 271-2343
800 / 258-3608 (from Northeast outside New Hampshire)

New Jersey

New Jersey Division of Travel and Tourism
Department of Commerce
C.N. 826
Trenton, NJ 08625
609 / 292-2470

New Mexico

New Mexico Travel Division
Economic Development and Tourism Department
Bataan Memorial Building
Santa Fe, NM 87503
505 / 827-6230
800 / 545-2040 (from outside New Mexico)

New York

New York State Division of Tourism
99 Washington Avenue
Albany, NY 12245
518 / 474-4116
800 / CALL NYS (from New England except Maine)

North Carolina

North Carolina Travel and Tourism Division
Department of Commerce
430 North Salisbury Street
Raleigh, NC 27611
919 / 733-4171
800 / VISIT NC (within No. Carolina)
800 / 847-4862 (from outside No. Carolina)

North Dakota

North Dakota Tourism Promotion
Liberty Memorial Building
Bismarck, ND 58505
701 / 224-2525
800 / 472-2100 (within No. Dakota)
800 / 437-2077 (from outside No. Dakota)

Ohio

Ohio Office of Travel & Tourism
P.O. Box 1001
Columbus, OH 43216
614 / 466-8844

Oklahoma

Oklahoma Division of Tourism
215 28th Street, N.E.
Oklahoma City, OK 73105
405 / 521-2409
800 / 522-8565 (within Oklahoma)
800 / 652-6552 (from neighboring states)

Oregon

Oregon Tourism Division
595 Cottage Street, N.E.
Salem, OR 97310
503 / 378-3451
800 / 233-3306 (within Oregon)
800 / 547-7842 (from outside Oregon)

Pennsylvania

Pennsylvania Bureau of Travel Development
Department of Commerce
416 Forum Building
Harrisburg, PA 17120
717 / 787-5453
800 / VISIT PA (from outside Pennsylvania)

Rhode Island

Rhode Island Department of Economic Development
Tourism Division
7 Jackson Walkway
Providence, RI 02903
401 277-2601
800 556-2484 (from outside Rhode Island—Maine to Virginia)

South Carolina

South Carolina Division of Tourism
P.O. Box 71
Columbia, SC 29202
803 / 758-2536

South Dakota

South Dakota Division of Tourism
State Capitol Building
Pierre, SD 57501
605 / 773-3301
800 / 952-2217 (within So. Dakota)
800 / 843-1930 (Tourism Dev. Office—within So. Dakota)

Tennessee

Tennessee Division of Tourist Development
P.O. Box 23170
Nashville, TN 37202
615 / 741-2158

Texas

Texas Tourist Development
P.O. Box 5064
Austin, TX 78763
512 / 465-7401

Utah

Utah Travel Council
Council Hall, Capitol Hill
Salt Lake City, UT 84114
801 / 533-5681

Vermont

Vermont Travel Division
134 State Street
Montpelier, VT 05602
802 / 828-3236

Virginia

Virginia State Travel Service
Ninth Street Office Building
202 No. 9th Street, Suite 500
Richmond, VA 23219
804 / 786-4484

Washington

Washington State Department of Commerce and Economic Development
Tourism Development Division
101 General Administration Building-AX 13
Olympia, WA 98504
206 / 753-5630
800 / 562-4570 (within Washington)
800 / 541-9274 (from outside Washington)

West Virginia

West Virginia Travel Development Division
Capitol Complex
Charleston, WV 25305
304 / 348-2286
800 / 624-9110

Wisconsin

Wisconsin Division of Tourism
P.O. Box 7606
Madison, WI 53707
608 / 266-2161
800 / 362-9566 (within Wisconsin)
800 / 372-2737 (from neighboring states)

Wyoming

Wyoming Travel Commission
Frank Norris, Jr. Travel Center
Cheyenne, WY 82002
307 / 777-7777

Index

We are always interested in hearing from our readers. Whether you are beginning or already established as a host or RSO operator, we welcome your comments. And, of course, if you wish us to include your RSO or guidebook in our next edition, send the relevant information to us at Box 122, Spencertown, NY 12165.

From Maine to California, here's what they're saying . . .

"Since ordering your book a couple of weeks ago I've told a number of people to contact you to order a copy for themselves. We get lots of inquiries from people who either are just starting—or want to start—their own B&B. Your book is full of good, sensible, useful information—the best one on the subject I've seen."

Sally B. Godfrey,Director,
Bed & Breakfast Down East, Ltd.,
(Eastbrook, Maine)

"At last, here's a book with both substance and readibility. A complete, well-organized guide to opening your home as a B&B."

Beverly Walsh, Director,
The American Country Collection of
B&Bs, (NY, VT, MA) (Schenectady, NY)

"Your new book was the perfect addition to the seminar conducted last week. It offers complete coverage of areas to consider, details for each host to examine in order to run a smooth B&B, and directness—all the things I like when reading a subject for information and help. I especially liked the information about taxes, insurance, zoning. This area is so contradictory that most people remain confused even after discussion. Much success with your new publication."

Judy Antico, Seminar Teacher and
Director, Pittsburgh B&B Reservation
Service, (Pittsburgh, Pennsylvania)

"Your book arrived last week and I found it enjoyable and informative. I will be happy to offer it to my hosts and others considering B&B hosting."

Eileen Wood, Bed & Breakfast
Guest Homes, (Algoma, Wisconsin)

"Your book was just what was needed to help tell the Bed & Breakfast story. Both prospective Hosts and Guests will find it very helpful and it is so easy to read. I am so happy to recommend it to all who inquire".

Wilma Bloom, Director,
Bed & Breakfast, in Iowa, Ltd.,
(Preston, Iowa)

"Excellent hints and check lists for anyone considering opening their own home for B&B guests; including good support advice about RSOs."

Kate Peterson Winters,
Coordinator, B&B Rocky Mountains,
(CO, WY, UT, NM, MT) (Co. Spr., CO)

"The book is well-written, simple and clear. It covers the things that we, as RSO operators, take for granted and assume that prospective hosts know, when they may not. This book tells them the common-sense basics."

Alex Laputz, Director,
Bed & Breakfast Homestay,
(Cambria, California)

Mary Zander lived in New York's Greenwich Village before moving to a historic hamlet near the Hudson River Valley and the Massachusetts Berkshires. Her career has taken her traveling around the United States, whence she has come to appreciate B&Bs as a pleasant alternative to the motel/hotel circuit. She now operates her own B&B in an 18th century saltbox cottage. She has worked with the local Chamber of Commerce to encourage B&B in her area, and has taught seminars advising beginning hosts in several other states as well.